THE CASE FOR
TEACHING CREATION

KNOW the TRUTH BOOKS

The Bible Study Textbook Series

NEW TESTAMENT

The Bible Study New Testament Ed. By Rhoderick Ice	**The Gospel of Matthew** In Four Volumes By Harold Fowler (Vol. IV not yet available)	**The Gospel of Mark** By B. W. Johnson and Don DeWelt
The Gospel of Luke By T. R. Applebury	**The Gospel of John** By Paul T. Butler	**Acts Made Actual** By Don DeWelt
Romans Realized By Don DeWelt	**Studies in Corinthians** By T. R. Applebury	**Guidance From Galatians** By Don Earl Boatman
The Glorious Church (Ephesians) By Wilbur Fields	**Philippians · Colossians Philemon** By Wilbur Fields	**Thinking Through Thessalonians** By Wilbur Fields
Paul's Letters To Timothy & Titus By Don DeWelt	**Helps From Hebrews** By Don Earl Boatman	**James & Jude** By Don Fream
Letters From Peter By Bruce Oberst	**Hereby We Know (I-II-III John)** By Clinton Gill	**The Seer, The Saviour, and The Saved (Revelation)** By James Strauss

OLD TESTAMENT

O.T. History By William Smith and Wilbur Fields	**Genesis** In Four Volumes By C. C. Crawford	**Exploring Exodus** By Wilbur Fields	**Leviticus** By Don DeWelt
Numbers By Brant Lee Doty	**Deuteronomy** By Bruce Oberst	**Joshua · Judges Ruth** By W. W. Winter	**I & II Samuel** By W. W. Winter
I & II Kings By James E. Smith	**I & II Chronicles** By Robert E. Black	**Ezra, Nehemiah & Esther** By Ruben Ratzlaff & Paul T. Butler	**The Shattering of Silence (Job)** By James Strauss
Psalms In Two Volumes By J. B. Rotherham	**Proverbs** By Donald Hunt		**Ecclesiastes and Song of Solomon** — By R. J. Kidwell and Don DeWelt
Isaiah In Three Volumes By Paul T. Butler	**Jeremiah and Lamentations** By James E. Smith		**Ezekiel** By James E. Smith
Daniel By Paul T. Butler	**Hosea · Joel · Amos Obadiah · Jonah** By Paul T. Butler		**Micah · Nahum · Habakkuk Zephaniah · Haggai · Zechariah Malachi** — By Clinton Gill

SPECIAL STUDIES

The Church In The Bible By Don DeWelt	**The Eternal Spirit** By C. C. Crawford	**World & Literature of the Old Testament** Ed. By John Willis	**Survey Course In Christian Doctrine** Two Bks. of Four Vols. By C. C. Crawford
New Testament History — Acts By Gareth Reese	**Learning From Jesus** By Seth Wilson		**You Can Understand The Bible** By Grayson H. Ensign

KNOW THE TRUTH BOOKS

THE CASE FOR TEACHING CREATION

By

A. J. Hoover

College Press Publishing Company, Joplin, Missouri

Library of Congress Catalog Card Number: 81-66952
International Standard Book Number: 0-89900-142-4

To Gloria, who defines what the word
"partner" means (Genesis 2:20).

THE CASE FOR TEACHING CREATION

And what is this God? I asked the earth and it answered: "I am not He"; and all things that are in the earth made the same confession. I asked the sea and the deeps and the creeping things, and they answered: "We are not your God; seek higher." I asked the winds that blow, and the whole air with all that is in it answered: "Anaximenes was wrong; I am not God." I asked the heavens, the sun, the moon, the stars, and they answered: "Neither are we God whom you seek." And I said to all the things that throng about the gateways of the senses: "Tell me of my God, since you are not He. Tell me something of Him." And they cried out in a great voice: "He made us."

Augustine, *Confessions,* X, vi.

PREFACE

The enthusiastic reception of my little book, *Fallacies of Evolution,* encouraged me to do additional research into the current creation-evolution controversy. In the spring of 1979 I participated in two public debates on the question, one in Portland, Oregon (March 15) and one in Concord, California (May 1, 2). In both discussions the proposition was, "Resolved: Evolution is the only theory of origins that should be taught in the public schools." Naturally I was in the negative.

The present work arose out of the thinking and research I did for these two debates. I think the American people are gradually inching toward a more equitable approach to the handling of origins and other metaphysical issues in the public schools. If this book contributes to an improved public understanding of the crucial issues involved in this controversy I will be satisfied.

It has been well over a century now since Charles Darwin kicked off this controversy with his *Origin of Species* (1859). Since that time western man has tried to view evolution as a confirmed scientific theory and teach it as such. By now, it should be obvious that this attempt to settle evolution permanently into the house of knowledge has failed. It is time to surrender the problem of origins back to metaphysics.

I am grateful to Dr. J. D. Thomas of the Biblical Research Press in Abilene, Texas, for allowing me to use portions of my books, *Fallacies of Unbelief* and *Ideas and Their Consequences,* and to Baker Book House, Grand Rapids, Michigan, for permission to use material from *Dear Agnos: A Defense of Christianity* and *Fallacies of Evolution.*

A. J. Hoover
Abilene Christian University
Abilene, Texas

1

INTRODUCTION

What should we teach about origins? Creation? Evolution? Both? Neither?

This question has agitated the educational world since the early 1960's. It waxes and wanes from time to time, it disturbs now one state and now another, but it won't go away. Champions of creation have vowed that they will not let the matter rest until the public schools have adopted a "two-model approach" to the problem of origins, that is, until we have a policy of teaching both creation and evolution when origins is discussed.

I happen to be one of those many champions of creationism. I feel that the present policy of teaching only evolution is wrong because the problem of origins is still an open question. No one has settled the question with solid, decisive, definitive evidence. And when a question is still open you dare not teach just one theory when two theories are possible. When you do that you prejudice the minds of your students. You just happen to teach what the stronger group forces you to teach. Our educational philosophy then becomes merely, "Might makes right!" We are then no better than Nazi Germany or Soviet Russia in our pedagogy.

I beg the reader to start this book with an open mind. I am *not* just beating the drums for the Christian religion, although I won't mind at all if my arguments redound to the glory of Jesus Christ or the Bible. But I am primarily arguing a case for science, for the scientific method. One of the finest things about the scientific method is the rigorous standard of proof it demands of all its theories. Creationists are asking that we apply that same rigorous standard of proof to the theory of evolution and see if it can take it. I claim that it can't.

Before we're finished with this topic it will become very clear that the words science and scientific are used very loosely in our times. The most prevalent objection to teaching creation is that it isn't truly a scientific theory, but rather a religious belief. This objection assumes that the general public instantly knows what the terms *scientific* and *religious* mean and that they know the distinction between them. As a matter of fact, most people use the terms so loosely that no intelligent discussion on the topic could occur until they are defined.

For the sake of clarity, I suggest that we employ two phrases in this study, "strict science" and "loose science."

1. By strict science I mean the classical scientific method rigorously applied, so rigorously applied that one could use the term knowledge of the results. Strict science desires to have direct empirical contact by an observer of an entity, process, or event. Strict science desires to have experimentation and

repetition of the event or process in question. When a theory reaches the status of a law it implies that the result is so certain that experimenters all around the world can work the same experiment and get the same results.

2. By loose science I mean a less rigorous, less conclusive, use of the scientific method. You use loose science when you suggest a hypothesis to correlate a body of data, when you argue a theory from circumstantial evidence, when you build up a case on inferential material. One can see science in the loose sense operating in a court of law. A good lawyer can't reproduce the event he's trying to prove ("Jones killed Brown") but he can show that all the evidence points to that conclusion. He builds a cogent scenario; he makes the jury "see" the event *through* the data. He argues, "Jones must be guilty because that is the only possible way to explain all this incriminating evidence." If the lawyer does his job well, the jury will have no regrets when they pronounce Jones guilty.

In a word, strict science means roughly *observation*, while loose science refers to *inference*.

It's true that strict and loose science are both parts of the classic scientific method; however, this distinction is still accurate and helpful, especially when we approach questions that can't be settled by the strict scientific approach.

Origins is such a question! This means not only the origins of animal forms but the origins of life itself and even the origins of the entire universe. Whatever happened, creation or evolution, or possibly both, it happened a long, long time ago. No one was there to observe it — no eyewitness, no scientist, no newspaper reporter, no photographer. We can't go back in a time machine to check any theory of origins. We can't experiment today to settle what happened long ago.

3

What this means is that origins will forever be a question of loose science; there is no way that strict science can handle it. We are doomed to argue from inference, not from direct observation. Origins, therefore, is a question kin to history, because you can never get at the event *directly.* You can only approach the event *indirectly,* through inferential data.

Now, all this may sound trite, but many evolutionists and many lay people don't seem to recognize this distinction. Many evolutionists talk as if evolution were as clearly established as the Law of Gravity or Boyle's Law of Gases. Many people think that if science should create life in the laboratory today that would settle how life originated long ago. This simply isn't true. Creating life today does not at all settle how life first began. The one is contemporary science; the other is past history. You don't settle past history by contemporary experiment. The most you prove is what *might* have happened in the past, not what really did happen. The question is still open.

If origins can't be settled by strict science, then it is open to two possible theories — creation and evolution. We therefore have an obligation to teach both theories, not just one. In the remainder of this study we will first, examine five options concerning the teaching of origins, second, present the scientific evidence for the creation model, and third, answer the most important objections to teaching evolution in the public schools.

2

WHAT TO TEACH?
THE FIVE POSSIBILITIES.

What should we teach about origins? The question con-
tains a slightly ambiguous word — *teach*. In ordinary English
teach means to cause someone to know a subject, to impart
information or skill, to assist someone in mastering a body
of fact. When you discuss a question that is open, however,
the word teach takes on a different meaning. With an open
question, teach means to suggest a possible hypothesis, to
cover and discuss all plausible explanations of a problem.

For example, I teach European intellectual history and I
must therefore cover such ideologies as Marxism, Com-
munism, Social Darwinism, Nihilism, Racism, and Fascism.
These are ideologies that I passionately reject but I can
teach them nevertheless. I can explain to a student what
Marxism claims without being a Marxist myself or without
implying that it is fact. I can present Marxism as a possible

model for the interpretation of social and economic processes — because it *is* a possible model. I can describe the arguments for it and give some arguments against it. But in all this teaching of Marxism I am not offering it as a strict science, because it does not yet enjoy that status, and probably never will. It is still a model, a theory, a hypothesis.

The same is true with creation and evolution. Since origins is an open question we should not teach either as fact. We should discuss both, examine both, present the evidence for both, but let the student decide for himself what is true, or let him perhaps suspend judgment on the matter of origins.

Here again, we may compare origins with an event in history, let us say, for example, the assassination of President John F. Kennedy in 1963. The Warren Commission concluded that the President was killed by a lone assassin and that there was no conspiracy. Many students of the same data have since challenged that conclusion. One could not teach the conclusion of the Warren Commission as established fact because it is still theory — a good theory, but still theory. If you taught anything on the subject you would have to cover all the relevant data and then suggest which position, in your opinion, explained the data best.

Now, when it comes to teaching origins, there are five possible positions you can take. Let us examine each of these in turn, ending with the one this book will defend.

TEACH ONLY CREATION

Up until Charles Darwin, and even later in some places, creation, as set forth in the Jewish-Christian Scriptures (Genesis 1, 2), was the only theory of origins taught in school, public or private. This view states that all of the universe came into existence about six to ten thousand years ago by the creative act of a personal deity who accomplished this tremendous feat in six literal days.

After Darwin, evolution gradually began to make its way into the curriculum — as well it should. Any theory of origins that can give a plausible explanation of the data of origins deserves to be investigated alongside creation. A few years ago such a statement would have disturbed many creationists, but even the most dedicated creationist nowadays freely admits that evolution has a right to be taught alongside creation. We don't desire to return to pre-Scopes days; no one wants to ban Darwin's *Origin of Species* or jail anyone who teaches it. Teaching creation exclusively is a practice that few creationists will wish to restore. Even in private religious colleges, science teachers should present evolution, if for no other reason than to expose students to an alternative model.

TEACH ONLY EVOLUTION

In general, the present policy in the western world is to teach only evolution when the question of origins is discussed. Some evolutionists teach the theory in a theoretical vein, others dish it out as cold, hard fact. If origins is an open question, if no solid, definitive data exists to close the question in favor of evolution, then this policy is a pedagogical crime. It is an affront against the academic rights of students, who deserve to hear both sides when a question is open.

It is surprising that educators don't insist on presenting only one side of a question in hardly any other discipline. In psychology, for instance, when a moot issue like *personality* is studied, the student is encouraged to investigate several schools of thought — Psychoanalysis, Behaviorism, Logotherapy, or Reality Therapy. Such a course is sometimes called, "Theories of Personality," usually accompanied by a textbook of the same title.[1] The course and text will cover figures as diverse as Freud and Maslow, Skinner and Allport, Pavlov and Fromm.

Why can't this be done in the study of origins? Isn't origins just as moot, just as speculative, just as open as the problem of personality? Why couldn't we have a course entitled, "Theories of Origins"?

Even Clarence Darrow of Scopes trial fame remarked that it is "bigotry for public schools to teach only one theory of origins."

TEACH NEITHER CREATION NOR EVOLUTION

Some people despair at solving this problem and conclude that we should teach neither creation nor evolution. Don't even bring up the question of origins in the schools, they say, just teach the hard facts that you can confirm perfectly by strict laboratory technique and let the students get anything else from some other institution.

As a matter of judicial fact, the state has power to remove instruction in a particular subject from a public school course. In *Mercer* v. *Michigan State Board of Education* (1974) a federal district court upheld the exclusion of sex education courses and of birth control from biology courses. The judges in the *Mercer* decision noted that, "The authorities must choose which portions of the world's knowledge will be included in the curriculum's programs and courses, and which portions will be left for grasping from other sources. . . ."[2]

---

1. See, for example, Richard M. Ryckman, *Theories of Personality* (New York: Nostrand, 1978); Calvin S. Hall and Gardner Lindzey, *Theories of Personality* (New York: Wiley, 1957).

2. Cited in Wendell R. Bird, "Freedom of Religion and Science Instruction in Public Schools," *Yale Law Journal*, Vol. 87, No. 3 (January, 1978), p. 566.

While admitting the state's right to define curricular content, and while concurring that this approach would solve some knotty problems in the matter, I nevertheless feel that elimination of any discussion of origins altogether would be pedagogically cruel and unnecessary. Curiosity about origins is natural for man. At a very early age children begin to ask those troublesome questions about origins like, "Where did I come from?", "Where do babies come from?", or "Where did the world come from?" To prohibit any discussion at all of such questions would rob the students of a valuable learning experience. The students would be puzzled by such a prohibition and wonder about its rationale. (Imagine having to sneak around to study Darwin and Genesis!)

What we really want is *an arrangement where we encourage the student to investigate the problem of origins and at the same time help him to understand its unsettled status.* The next two positions come closer than the first three in achieving this result.

TEACH EVOLUTION BUT AVOID DOGMATISM

This view takes some careful explaining. Many evolutionists admit that origins is an unsettled question, yet they refuse to introduce what they consider a religious belief into science classes. So, they say, "Let's teach evolution, but teach it humbly, pointing out that it hasn't been proved yet, which leaves open the possibility of creation, or perhaps of theistic evoluton." They usually feel that evolution of animal forms is more certain than the spontaneous generation of life, and both of these are more amenable to scientific treatment than the origins of the entire universe. They admit that the ultimate origin of matter and energy is almost pure speculation, sheer metaphysics.

When you get to metaphysics, say these people, you are so far beyond good science that you *must* be humble. You must not commit the error of *scientism,* which is to assume that Naturalism or Materialism are logical corollaries of the scientific method. Scientism tends to reduce all reality to the mere empirical world and make the empirical scientific method the only touchstone for truth. It commits what we call the Reductive Fallacy, because it reduces all reality to matter or empirical reality, thus prejudicing the case for Materialism. We must commend the people holding this position for their clear perception of the dangers of scientism and reductionism.[3]

Some Christians prefer this solution to the origins teaching impasse. For instance, Dr. Richard Bube of Stanford University, editor of the *Journal of the American Scientific Affiliation,* affirms that teaching creation would violate the integrity of both science and religious faith. He agrees with the creationist that, "If science courses offer *ultimate* explanations for origins, then these explanations *should* be deleted. If science courses offer possible mechanism for the origin of life and man in the form of scientific descriptions of historical events, this is right and proper."[4] But, against the creationist, he says that it is not science that must be held in check but rather misinterpretations or extrapolations of science into non-scientific realms. He accuses the creationist of not appreciating the possibility that creation and evolution are "two alternative *modes of description* of origins, that, in fact, these two descriptions complement one another and do not contradict one another."[5]

---

3. See my *Fallacies of Evolution* (Baker, 1977), for a more detailed analysis of various fallacies committed by evolutionists. T. H. Huxley illustrates the spirit of scientism when he writes, "The laboratory is the fore-court of the temple of philosophy; and whoso has not offered sacrifices and undergone purification there, has little chance of admission into the sanctuary." (*Hume with Helps to the Study of Berkeley* [New York: D. Appleton and Co., 1896], p. 61).

4. *Journal of the American Scientific Affiliation,* Vol. 30, No. 2 (June, 1978), p. 96.

5. *Ibid.,* p. 97.

Dr. Bube's position is essentially that adopted by the California State Board of Education in 1973 after a stormy two-year battle over the question of what to allow in the textbooks. California must now follow these guidelines:

> . . . on the subject of discussing origins in the Science textbooks, the following edition [must] be done prior to execution of a contract (with a publisher): 1. That dogmatism be changed to conditional statements where speculation is offered as explanation for origins. 2. That science emphasize "how" and not "ultimate cause" for origins.[6]

Teaching evolution while avoiding metaphysics is certainly a viable solution to the problem of what to teach on origins. It is a significant improvement over the present policy of teaching only evolution. However, it still falls short of a completely equitable policy. Against it we urge the following objections:

1. It still prejudices the subject of origins toward Naturalism and Materialism. Even if you teach evolution with humility, if it is the *only* theory you teach, the net result on the mind of the student is to teach it as fact. This is especially true in the high school or grade school, where critical and analytical ability is not highly developed.[7]

2. Teaching evolution as a "possible mechanism" for the origins of things is misleading and deceptive unless you balance that teaching with other possible mechanisms. How does the student know it is merely "possible" unless he sees an alternative? It's difficult for you to assume that *methodological* naturalism won't become *metaphysical* naturalism in

---

6. *Ibid.*, p. 96. For some examples of how more recent texts have followed these guidelines, see D. Nelkin, "The Science-Textbook Controversies," *Scientific American*, Vol. 234, No. 4 (April, 1976), p. 38.

7. Marek and Renner report that "73 percent of the tenth-graders interviewed cannot do formal operational thinking" (*Science Teacher*, September, 1972, p. 32).

the mind of the student unless the instructor explicitly warns him that there is no necessary connection between the two.

3. Teaching evolution in humility leaves it up to the individual science teacher to prevent the inequity creationists complain about. Unfortunately, many science teachers, having been schooled in evolution, wouldn't feel any tremendous moral obligation to give the other theory if it's left up to them. It's easy to sound humble while you're still subtly implying that only one theory is really true. One biology teacher said bluntly, "They can't make me teach that d--- theory of creation!"

In summary, teaching evolution with humility still shows favoritism toward naturalistic evolution; the method favors the view that physical causes explain everything, it subtly preaches Humanism. Proof of this can be seen in the frantic attempts of the American Humanist Association to prevent the introduction of creation into the science curriculum.[8] Madalyn Murray O'Hair is also anxious to keep the science curriculum pure from all religious models of origins. When you notice all these apostles of Humanism becoming alarmed at the prospect of including creation in the science curriculum, you suspect that some favoritism is being shown.

TEACH BOTH CREATION AND EVOLUTION

In my judgment, teaching both creation and evolution is an idea whose time has come. Once we taught only creation, then we taught only evolution. Now it's time for us to realize that origins can't be settled by the strict scientific method.

---

8. See the AHA manifesto, "A Statement Affirming Evolution as a Principle of Science," *The Humanist,* January-February, 1977, Vol. XXXVII, p. 4. This document was signed by such scientific pillars as Isaac Asimov, Linus Pauling, George Gaylord Simpson, and 163 others.

Origins pushes you into the realm of metaphysics (philosophical views of reality) where you must exercise extreme caution in discussing a question. The First and Great Commandment in the realm of metaphysics is: "Thou shalt not pontificate!" The two-model approach which presents both creation and evolution obeys this commandment; the one-model approach which presents only evolution breaks it.

We strongly recommend the two-model approach for the following reasons:

1. *It is good science.* If a question is still open, then science classes should not suggest that it is closed. This would be disloyal to true science, because science at its best is humble when it comes to nature and to the mystery of existence. Elton Trueblood speaks to the point: "Science asks questions and accepts evidence of all kinds without judging the situation in advance. To say that we cannot know objective reality except by means of sense experience is clearly to prejudge the case. It is, therefore, unscientific."[9]

2. *It is good teaching method.* Even before actual studies were made of the question any good teacher could have told you that presenting two models on a body of data will help the student to understand every aspect of the problem — the data as well as both of the models.

Now, however, we have empirical confirmation of this premonition in studies conducted by Dr. Richard B. Bliss in California. Dr. Bliss and his associates conducted experiments to test the question of whether the two-model approach was superior in learning results to the one-model approach. The tests showed the two-model approach definitely superior. It turned out that the students studying both models did better in learning *all* the material, even the data and the arguments for evolution! "It would seem, then," Dr. Bliss

---

9. *Philosophy of Religion* (New York: Harper, 1957), p. 197.

concludes, "that it would be unconscionable from a pedagogical and scientific point of view, to teach only evolution to students in the public high schools."[10]

3. *It is good legal practice.* Teaching both creation and evolution is a legal possibility, *if* creation can be shown to be a genuine scientific model, the burden of our next chapter. Every serious participant in this discussion should secure the article by Wendell R. Bird, "Freedom of Religion and Science Instruction in Public Schools," *Yale Law Journal,* Volume 87, No. 3, January, 1978, pp. 515-570.[11] In this learned article, which won the Egger Prize for 1978, Mr. Bird argues cogently that teaching evolution as the only theory violates the "free exercise" clause of the First Amendment, which reads, "Congress shall make no law respecting an establishment of religion, or prohibiting the free exercise thereof." Bird shows that teaching evolution exclusively inhibits the free exercise of religion by teaching as fact a theory of origins that contradicts the faith of most students in school.

We will have to take this matter up again when we investigate several objections to teaching creation.

Now we must turn to the critical question: Is creation a viable scientific model, worthy of parallel treatment with evolution in the science curriculum?

---

10. Bliss, *Origins: Two Models — Evolution and Creation* (San Diego, California: Creation-Life Publishers, 1976).

11. The reader may obtain this article by sending $2.50 to Drawer 401A, Yale Station, Yale University, New Haven, Connecticut, 06520.

3

THE CREATION MODEL OF ORIGINS

Evolutionists usually oppose the teaching of creation in the public schools because, they insist, it is not science but theology or religion. The purpose of this chapter is to show that creation is a viable model for origins and that by any fair definition of the word *theory,* creation is a scientific theory. In chapter five we will re-examine the traditional distinction between science and theology.

Many creationists now use the phrase, "scientific creationism," to distinguish the generic creation model from any specific account of creation taught in a religious document like the book of Genesis.[1] If we taught creation simply as it comes from the Bible we would run afoul of court decisions resting on the separation of church and state. But if we offer creation simply as a possible scientific model we do not

1. At present the definitive work on the topic is *Scientific Creationism,* edited by Henry M. Morris (San Diego, California: Creation-Life Publishers, 1974).

violate the separation of church and state, as long as that separation is fairly interpreted.

WHAT IS A SCIENTIFIC THEORY?

The word theory comes from a Greek word, *theoreo,* which means "I behold," or "I perceive." A theory, therefore, is something conceptual, something I conceive or comprehend, something I behold in a conceptual sense, not in a direct empirical sense. You don't see a theory in the same sense you see the data it explains. A theory is a concept that unifies and interrelates the facts of observation. It is an understanding, a comprehension that imposes order or meaning upon a body of data.

This analogy will help: the facts of observation are like the pieces of a jig-saw puzzle, while the theory is the picture that emerges when you get all the pieces together. Furthermore, even before you finish the puzzle the picture helps you to fit the pieces together. The puzzle would take a very long time to work if you fitted the pieces together by looking at the shapes instead of the picture. Likewise, a good theory will suddenly interrelate pieces of observation that you might have thought were totally unrelated.

To vary the metaphor, devising a good theory is like throwing a magnet into a pile of metal scraps. The pieces of metal suddenly turn toward the magnet and arrange themselves into a pattern. In the same manner a theory causes the facts of experience to turn toward it and arrange themselves in a special way, into a paradigm that satisfies the intellect.

A good theory accomplishes three things:

1. It explains the facts of observation. It throws the data into a configuration that makes sense to the mind.

2. It points to new areas of research. It opens up new avenues of observation. If it is a good theory, the new data it uncovers tend to support the original theory.

3. It allows you to make predictions of the future that check with experience by testing. For example, the discovery of the planet Neptune helped confirm the law of gravity and Newtonian mechanics because its existence had been predicted as a necessary consequent of the theory.

So far, I can't see anything about a theory of origins that would rule out a creative deity. Someone may reply that since God is invisible or non-empirical He couldn't function as a theory, but this objection would also eliminate many things that were first postulated but not seen — atoms, genes, radium, germs, Neptune. Carlo Lastrucci writes:

> A theory . . . is a generalized, synthetic explanatory statement of the "cause" of a phenomenon or of the interrelation between classes of phenomena. As such, it often employs abstractions having no apparent empirical qualities (e.g. "force," "symbiosis," "intelligence," "social mobility"). Its function is to serve as the unifying explanation for an unlimited series of possible deducible hypotheses; just as it may "explain" — or systematically account for — the relationship among laws.[2]

If intelligence can function as a scientific theory, what would be wrong with a creative intelligence (= God) functioning as a theory? In 1950 British astronomer Fred Hoyle proposed a strange cosmological theory called "Continuous Creation," also known as the "Steady-State Theory." Hoyle defended it by saying:

> This may seem a strange idea and I agree that it is, but in science it does not matter how strange an idea may seem so

2. *The Scientific Approach: Basic Principles of the Scientific Method* (Cambridge, Mass.: Schenkman Pub. Co., 1963), p. 15.

long as it works — that is to say, so long as the idea can be expressed in a precise form and so long as its consequences are found to be in agreement with observation.[3]

It would seem, then, that only an unfair definition of the quality of the entity theorized could eliminate God as a scientific theory. To reject God as strange or non-empirical is not enough. Hence, Norman D. Newell thrashes at a strawman when he complains that "at a juncture when science and technology have split the atom, cracked the gentic code, and put men on the moon, the current revival of pre-Darwinian theory has an eerie, dreamlike quality."[4] The adjectives, "pre-Darwinian," "eerie," and "dreamlike," are totally irrelevant to the discussion, mere emotive terms designed to prejudice the case against creation before the discussion can even get started.

THE CREATION MODEL

What, then, are the data that support creation? What features of the universe indicate the operation of deity? What facts of observation can be explained by a creative intelligence? We shall investigate eight of them:

1. The Stability of the Laws of Science
2. The First Law of Thermodynamics
3. The Second Law of Thermodynamics
4. The Fact of Biogenesis
5. The Permanence of Basic Kinds of Animals
6. The Mystery of the Cambrian Rocks
7. The Missing Transitional Forms
8. The Phenomenon of Design in the Universe

---

3. See chapter 6, originally entitled, "The Expanding Universe," in Hoyle's book, *The Nature of the Universe* (New York: Harper, 1950), p. 124.
4. "Evolution under Attack," *Natural History* (April, 1974), p. 37.

It will soon become apparent that many of these points are problems for the theory of evolution. This is not surprising, for the problems of one theory often become the strengths of another theory. This is especially true if you have only two theories in the field, which seems to be the case with the problem of origins.

1. The Stability of the Laws of Science

As far as we can tell, the cosmos we inhabit is a *universe*, not a *multi*verse, that is, it seems that the cosmos is all of one piece, having the same, uniform laws operating throughout. Moreover, these laws appear to be stable, not evolving. I say "appear" to be stable, because no one could guarantee that they might not change the second you finish reading this sentence! However, for all practical purposes, we may confidently assert that, "There is not as yet the slightest observational intimation that these entities are evolving at all."[5]

In fact, the constancy of matter/energy is so obvious that two of our most important laws in science are principles of conservation — (1) the Law of Mass Conservation and (2) the Law of Energy Conservation. This is exactly what you would expect and predict if a creation model were true. On the other hand, if evolution were true you would expect matter/energy and laws to be changing and developing.

Of course, the evolutionist may say that things *seem* stable now but that they have actually changed greatly in the past. He may say this, but the point is that his theory must *explain away* the present stability of things while the creation model predicts it! Stability follows necessarily from the creation model but stability is a problem for the evolution model.

---

5. Morris, *Scientific Creationism*, p. 18.

We shall find this pattern repeated throughout our list of eight features.

Further, by admitting that things are stable now, the evolutionist removes his theory from the arena of confirmable observation. He concedes that the burden of proof for change and development is on him, since the *prima facie* case favors stability. He thus removes his theory from the realm of strict science to the realm of loose science.

2. The First Law of Thermodynamics

If God created everything in an initial unit of time and then rested, and if God made a world that was perfect and complete, you would expect the operation of a principle of conservation to insure the accomplishment of the Creator's purpose for all created things.

The universe seems to behave exactly as you would expect if a creation had taken place. The First Law of Thermodynamics is a principle of conservation. It says that the amount of energy in the universe is constant though it changes in form; the amount is constant but not necessarily usable. Energy can be converted from one form to another, but can't be created or destroyed. This is what you would expect if a given quantum of energy had been called into existence at the very beginning of all things.

How certain is the First Law? Isaac Asimov claims that, "This law is considered the most powerful and most fundamental generalization about the universe that scientists have ever been able to make."[6]

We must admit that the idea of the creation of the total quantity of energy at one time in the past is only one possible theory of creation. The church father, Origen, for example,

---

6. "In the Game of Energy and Thermodynamics You Can't Even Break Even," *Journal of Smithsonian Institute* (June, 1970), p. 6.

held to the idea that God continually creates. Present science, however, prefers to believe that everything came into existence at once, in a "Big Bang" explosion about 20 billion years ago. The concept of a Big Bang is not incompatible with the notion of creation.

3. The Second Law of Thermodynamics

If the First Law defines the *quantity* of energy, the Second Law describes its *quality*. The fact that the amount of energy is always constant does not mean that energy is always available, no more than the fact that a clock will always weigh the same proves that it will keep on ticking forever. There is a continual downward use of energy, a diffusion, a dissipation of energy going on. Every day we live there is a net decrease in the available energy of the universe.

To state it simply: some bodies are hotter than others, and heat constantly flows from the hotter ones to the cooler ones. Heat automatically and spontaneously flows from a hot body to a cold body, not the reverse. If this process goes on for a few billion more years — and scientists have never observed a restoration of dissipate energy — then the result of the process will be a final state of thermal equilibrium, a "heat death," a random degradation of energy throughout the entire cosmos. This will mean the stagnation of all physical activity. The Second Law says, in effect, let things alone and they will go from bad to worse — iron will rust, flowers will wither, colors will fade, men will die, suns will burn out, everything will degenerate.[7]

Once again, this feature of the universe, the downward use of energy, is what you would expect if creation occurred,

---

7. See Asimov, *ibid.*; Harold F. Blum, *Time's Arrow and Evolution* (Princeton, N.J.: Princeton University Press, 1962), p. 14.

if a given quantity of energy were made at the beginning and started on its downward utilization process.

Does the Second Law make evolution impossible? Creationists are divided on this question. Some, like William W. Watts, warn that we must not use the Second Law so indiscriminately that we destroy such things as "life, birth, growth, springtime, resurrection and any other form of creativity."[8] Others, like Henry Morris and Duane Gish, argue that it makes spontaneous generation of life virtually impossible.[9]

One thing seems certain: the Second Law makes one very skeptical of the possibility of "total evolution," the kind of evolution that goes "from everlasting to everlasting," from primal matter to contemporary man. We see the contours of such evolutionism in Julian Huxley:

> Evolution in the extended sense can be defined as directional and essentially irreversible process occurring in time, which in its course gives rise to an increase of variety and an increasingly high level of organization in its products. Our present knowledge indeed forces us to the view that the whole of reality is evolution — a single process of self-transformation.[10]

The whole of reality is evolution! This is total evolution, the metaphysical kind of evolution rendered very unlikely by the Second Law of Thermodynamics. The reason it is unlikely is that energy is running down, not up. That is, if total evolution were true you would expect to find an eternal principle of innovation and complexification in all things. If random matter slowly develops into elements, stars, proteins, cells, worms, fishes, amphibians, reptiles,

---

8. "Ten Reasons Many Scientists Reject Creationism," *Liberty* (March-April, 1979), p. 6.
9. See Morris, *Scientific Creationism,* ch. 4.
10. *What is Science?* (New York: 1955).

mammals, and finally man, then some powerful principle of integration is obviously at work. But physics reveals no such principle at work; on the contrary it shows disintegration at work.

The two laws of thermodynamics definitely fit creation better than evolution. Evolution suggests *innovation* and *integration,* but the facts favor creation because they point to *conservation* (First Law) and *disintegration* (Second Law).

Now, it is curious to note that one of Darwin's mentors, Charles Hutton, had a faulty understanding of these laws. This was because the laws of thermodynamics, especially the second, were not clearly understood until the end of the last century. Consequently we're not surprised when Hutton says that, "The result, therefore, of our present enquiry is that we find no vestige of a beginning — no prospect of an end." The Second Law surely gives us today a "prospect of an end"![11]

4. The Fact of Biogenesis

Biogenesis means that life comes from pre-existing life. The General Theory of Evolution is naturalistic and materialistic; it requires the mechanical and accidental origins of all things from eternal matter with no supernatural intervention. It, therefore, requires spontaneous generation, the accidental origins of life from inert elements. Evolutionists think that such an event occurred about 3.5 billion years ago. This event is often spoken of in science classes as if it could be confirmed as easily as the boiling point of water.

What is the empirical evidence of spontaneous generation? Very little. There is a great deal of hopeful research

---

11. In his *Energy and Matter,* Louis Büchner, another nineteenth-century materialist, claimed that, "Matter is immortal and for this reason it is impossible that the world can have been created."

going on at present, but so far no solid evidence exists for the theory. As far as we can tell, life always comes from life, just as the creation model would predict.

G. A. Kerkut is unusually candid on the speculative nature of evolutionary theory at this point. "It is . . . a matter of faith on the part of the biologist that biogenesis did occur and he can choose whatever method of biogenesis happens to suit him personally; the evidence for what did happen is not available." He concludes with this apt observation: "It seems at times as if many of our modern writers on evolution have had their views by some sort of revelation."[12]

In 1973 I participated in a debate with an evolutionist at the University of California, Davis. We got into a vigorous discussion on the spontaneous generation of life from inert chemicals. One student pressed the evolutionist, "But how do you know it really happened?" The scientist replied: "Well, we're here, aren't we?" This answer commits a common fallacy known as *asserting the consequent*. The argument runs like this:

1. If spontaneous generation of life occurred, then we would be here.
2. We are here.
3. Therefore, spontaneous generation of life occurred.

You can see that the creationist could make the same argument with equal force:

1. If creation occurred, we would be here.
2. We are here.
3. Therefore, creation occurred.

In other words, we would be here regardless of which occurred — creation or evolution! Many diseases have the same symptoms. Several causes may have the exact same

12. *Implications of Evolution* (Oxford: Pergamon Press, 1965), p. 150.

results. Asserting the consequent is a fallacy, therefore, because you can't always tell how many different causes exist for the same consequent or result.

Now, I was stunned to find that many highly-trained scientists fall into this fallacy. In his *Physics and Chemistry of Life,* Harvard professor George Wald admits that spontaneous generation of life is impossible, yet it happened! How do we know? Because we're here! "Time is the hero of the plot," Wald demands. "However improbable we regard this event, or any of the steps which it involves, given enough time, it will almost certainly happen at least once." Without offering a shred of evidence for this wild assertion, he continues, "The time with which we have to deal is of the order of two billion years. What we regard as impossible on the basis of human experience is meaningless here. Given so much time, the 'impossible' becomes possible, the possible probable, and the probable virtually certain. One has only to wait; time itself performs the miracles."[13]

I thought we religionists were the only ones who believed in miracles. Professor Wald says that time performs miracles. He reminds you of those Kerkut mentions who "have had their views by some sort of revelation." Why does Wald believe in spontaneous generation, even though it seems impossible? Presumably because, as he says in another place, "the only alternative to some form of spontaneous generation is a belief in supernatural creation."[14]

---

13. (New York: Simon & Schuster, 1955), p. 12. Similarly, Robert Silverberg says, "Through some miracle that we may never understand chemical substances came together and took on the mysterious qualities we call life" (*Forgotten by Time: A Book of Living Fossils,* New York: Crowell, 1966, p. 23).

14. "Innovation in Biology," *Scientific American,* Vol. 199 (September, 1958), p. 100.

Exactly why is the theistic alternative so repugnant to this scientist? Why can't he at least suspend judgment on the matter and agree with Kerkut that "the evidence for what did happen is not available"? The way some evolutionists reason on the question of origins makes you agree with Aldous Huxley: "It is highly unfortunate that so few scientists are ever taught anything about the metaphysical foundations of science."[15]

It would seem, then, that the facts once again fit creation better than evolution. Life comes from life and whoever asserts the contrary has the burden of proof. One would have to admit, however, that if this were the only point under consideration we should just suspend judgment on origins. If we end up preferring creation, it will be because there is an accumulation of different kinds of evidence. We will end up preferring the model with the most explanatory power.

5. The Permanence of Basic Kinds of Animals

The creation model would lead you to believe that the basic kinds[16] of animals are stable, with no radical changes occurring in their essential structure. The evolution model requires you to think that radical changes have occurred in animal structures over millions of years of earth history.

At this point our discussion can't proceed until we make a crucial distinction between two kinds of evolution, macroevolution and microevolution.

---

15. *Ends and Means* (New York: Harper, 1937), p. 298.

16. One should note carefully that Biblical scholars are not at all sure what the word "kind" meant in Genesis 1. It could have been roughly equivalent to our *species,* but some insist that it could have been as broad in meaning as *genus* or *family.* Even today the exact parameters of a species are the subject of hot dispute among biologists.

1. *Macroevolution* refers to the kind of radical change in life forms asserted by the General Theory of Evolution. Scientists sometimes refer to it as a journey from "matter to man" or "molecules to man" or "amoeba to man" or "particles to people." This view of life is of necessity naturalistic, non-theistic, materialistic, mechanistic, and deterministic.

2. *Microevolution,* on the other hand, refers simply to small changes in plant and animal forms that can be observed by contemporary science. Microevolution is an observed fact; it happens every time we develop a new rose or breed a new variety of dog. Since the word evolution is often misleading we should perhaps refer to this process by better terms such as *variation, mutation,* or *speciation.* This kind of evolution is not necessarily naturalistic. It does not rule out the possibility of a creation. It has no compelling metaphysical implications.

Please note carefully: microevolution is an observed fact, while macroevolution is an unproved theory. The trouble arises when evolutionists cite the facts of microevolution to prove the theory of macroevolution, a most reprehensible practice. One favorite case they cite is the peppered moth of England (*Biston betularia*), which has supposedly changed its color in the last century in response to the dirt and pollution of English cities. Actually it didn't really change its color, since the dark-colored moths were a minority part of the total population all along. Pollution caused the dark-colored moths to dominate because they survived thanks to their camouflage. In spite of all this, the moths are still *Biston betularia,* with no change having occurred in the basic species.

The same goes for the wonderfully varied finches of Galopagas Islands that mesmerized Darwin, as well as for the strange variations produced in the fruit fly. None of these examples of mutation is relevant to the question: Did insects arise from a non-insect form of life? Did finches arise from a non-avian form of life? Mutation, speciation, and variation do not provide an answer to that question.

You would expect that if evolution were true we would have more beneficial mutations, since this is the alleged mechanism that drives life upward in its eternal complexification. All geneticists, however, such as Goldschmidt, Winchester, Glass, and Müller, agree that 99% of all mutations are either neutral or lethal. Richard Goldschmidt reminds us that, "It is good to keep in mind . . . that nobody has ever succeeded in producing a new species, not to mention the higher categories, by selection of micro-mutations."[17] N. Heribert-Nilsson, onetime Director of the Swedish Botanical Institute (Lund, Sweden), described the species as "the supreme unit in nature," which, he adds, is constant. All other classifications are somewhat arbitrary except the species, since we have experimental evidence for its limits. We can produce many variations by manipulating existing gene pools but we have yet to produce a truly new kind of animal.

If anyone ever wanted solid proof for evolution it was Theodosius Dobzhansky and even he admitted that there was no experimental evidence for the theory from mutation.

These evolutionary happenings are unqiue, unrepeatable, and irreversible. It is as impossible to turn a land vertebrate into a fish as it is to effect the reverse transformation. The applicability of the experimental method to the study of such unique historical processes is severely restricted before all else by the time intervals involved, which far exceed the lifetime of any human experimenter. And yet it is just such impossibility that is demanded by antievolutionists when

17. *Theoretical Genetics* (University of California Press, 1955).

they ask for "proofs" of evolution which they would magnanimously accept as satisfactory.[18]

I'm glad Dobzhansky admits that the proof for evolution is "impossible" to produce by the experimental method and that one is forced to treat it as an historical problem. This is the main point creationists are trying to make. But when he says that we anti-evolutionists demand impossible proof, I reply, "No, not we, but the scientific method demands it!"

The mutation mechanism received a blow in 1967 from a group of mathematicians, all of whom were evolutionists, who insisted that it was possible to calculate by probability analysis how long it would take to convert an amoeba into a man. Assuming that small mutations are mechanically produced in a random chance manner, it would take very much longer than the five billion years of earth history evolutionists postulate. These analysts concluded that the randomness postulate was highly unlikely and that evolution needed a new mechanism.[19]

But the only other mechanism possible in evolutionary terms is mega-mutation, or chromosomal change, a sudden, drastic change of an animal into another basic kind of animal. This is an event which has never been observed and moreover, say most biologists, would surely kill the animal. Nevertheless, Dr. Richard Goldschmidt, disenchanted with the micro-mutation mechanism, proposed what he called "the hopeful monster mechanism." He suggested that at one time a reptile laid an egg and a bird hatched from it! Miracles again! Most evolutionists strongly disagree and point out that Goldschmidt has no evidence for such an event, but

---

18. "On Methods of Evolutionary Biology and Anthropology," *American Scientist,* Vol. 45 (December, 1957), p. 388.

19. See P. S. Moorhead and M. M. Kaplan, *Mathematical Challenges to the Neo-Darwinian Interpretation of Evolution* (Philadelphia: Wistar Institute Press, 1967).

Goldschmidt reponds by pointing out that there is likewise no evidence for neo-Darwinism, the micro-mutation mechanism. As Duane Gish remarks, the creationist sits on the sidelines in this dispute and agrees with both sides — *there is no evidence for either type of mutation.*[20]

It is simply a fact that we do not know of any mechanism that would provide change of the degree needed for progressive evolution. Once again, the knowledge we have — as opposed to speculation — favors creation.

Now we must go into the fossil record and ascertain whether it favors creation or evolution, or perhaps neither. It doesn't take you long in the study of the data to see that the crucial evidence lies in the fossil record. As Sir Julian Huxley said, if you can't prove evolution there, then all the other arguments are very weak.

The fossil record shows that various animal forms once existed that are now extinct and it seems to suggest that in certain cases there has been a gradual development of anatomical structures through successive stages from simple to complex. The evidence of fossils is good enough to cause the creationist to be cautious in saying that there have been no changes since the beginning — an idea that some maintain but which is not at all required by Scripture. Anyone who seriously suggests that the devil planted dinosaur bones in the earth to test the faith of believers makes the creationist position look ridiculous. Whatever the rocks prove, we should rejoice in the truth.

In keeping with our general theme — that origins is an open question and that no decisive evidence exists to close it — we feel an obligation to demonstrate the inconclusive nature of the fossil record. We should note how very sketchy,

---

20. *Evolution? The Fossils Say No!* (San Diego, CA.: Creation-Life Publishers, 1973), p. 119.

damaged, and incomplete the story of the rocks appears. Perhaps the greatest problem facing the paleontologist is that he has only the skeletal system to work with. He must reconstruct the rest of the animal's structure by inference from the skeleton. But even the skeleton can be drastically altered by things like dietary deficiencies, rickets, and pituitary giantism, making it even more difficult to reconstruct and classify the organism. Fossils have often been twisted and distorted by the great pressure of rocks upon them. They are often damaged and exposed by erosion.

Fossils can easily be misinterpreted. Some species are so varied that you might never be able to see the essential features of a species just from fossil remains. For example, all dogs, from the tiny Chihuahua to the St. Bernard, belong to just one species, *Canis familiaris*. But if you didn't know the dog as a modern species, if you knew it only from fossilized skeletons, you might conclude that you were dealing with a number of separate species.

As a source of decisive evidence the fossil record is very incomplete. We have millions of fossils, true, but they represent only a fraction of the many animals that lived in the past. J. H. Hamon compares the entire paleontological record to a 400-page novel in which we have only pages 13, 38, 170, 172, 340, and 400.[21] In addition, our existing fossils don't give us a true random sample of the types that have lived before. Most of our fossils are over-represented by organisms from shallow seas, swampy areas, river mouths, and bogs.

Evolutionists like to refer to the "geological column," but

---

21. Cited by John W. Klotz, "Creationist Viewpoints," *A Symposium on Creation* (Grand Rapids, Michigan: Baker Book House, 1968), p. 50.

this is a species of verbal legerdemain.[22] The metaphor "column" implies that the fossil record is intact and continuous, like a temple column, from Cambrian to modern times. This simply is not true. Nowhere on earth do you find a perfect column all the way from the earliest animal deposits to the present. Those neat little complete charts you see in the science textbooks are *theoretical reconstructions*. They are based on inference and could be wrong.

Furthermore, the geological layers are often out of sequence. Sometimes you find layers supposed to be recent lying right down on the "basement complex," the — alleged — bottom of the series. Sometimes layers that are supposed to be millions of years apart are found right next to each other, with no apparent reason how they got that way.[23] If evolution is a confirmed fact, it is indeed strange that we can't find a single case of a complete or even near-complete example of the geological column.

---

22. Another example of this word trickery is the use of "primitive" and "modern." An animal is sometimes called primitive if it is simple in structure and modern if it is complex, with no other independent line of evidence to establish its date.

23. A classic example of this is the famous Lewis Overthrust, located in southern Canada and coming down partly in Glacier National Park in Montana. Recent estimates make it 350 miles wide and six miles thick, with an estimated horizontal displacement of at least 35 or 40 miles. This slab of rock is believed to weigh about 800,000 billion tons! Yet it is essentially a monolith, as geologists would call it, or as much a monolith as you're likely to find in the earth's crust. The problem is that it's out of place, as far as evolutionary geology is concerned. The top half is Pre-Cambrian limestone, obviously laid down by tremendous water action, while the bottom half is Cretaceous rocks, which are supposed to be 500 million years younger. If such a monolith were truly thrust out of place it would have created a tremendous mass of broken rock in front of it and along the sides, but no such broken rock can be found. It would have taken so much force to move this slab vertically against the pull of gravity and laterally against the side friction that it would have shattered it into innumerable pieces. See Whitcomb and Morris, *The Genesis Flood* (Grand Rapids, Michigan: Baker, 1967), pp. 185-192.

It would appear, therefore, that the fossil record is not exactly a source of decisive evidence for evolution, as evolutionists often imply.[24] It reminds you of the District Attorney who stood up in court and said, "Ladies and gentlemen of the jury, the decisive evidence for the defendant's guilt comes from his house, but unfortunately his house just burned down!"

Let us now turn to two features of the fossil record that disturb the theory of evolution: the Cambrian rocks and the missing transitional forms.

6. The Mystery of the Cambrian Rocks

G. G. Simpson calls the situation in the Cambrian strata the major remaining mystery in the origins of life. In these oldest fossil-bearing rocks we find examples of almost all the major phyla of animals existing in the world today. More than 5000 species lie in the Cambrian strata and the most striking thing about them is that they are complex, not simple, as you would expect.

For example, in the Cambrian rocks we find groups like porifera, coelenterates, brachiopods, mollusca, echinoids, and arthropods. We find lamp shells, moss animals, sea cucumbers, worms, trilobites, and shrimp. These creatures had complex organs like intestines, stomachs, bristles, spines, and appendages. They had eyes and feelers, which indicates that they possessed a good nervous system. They had gills, which shows that they both extracted oxygen from the water and had complex blood circulation systems. Some of them grew by molting, a complicated process still not thoroughly understood by scientists. They had intricate mouthpieces

24. Carl Sagan, for instance, in his *Dragons of Eden* (New York: Ballentine Books, 1977), p. 6, says that the fossil record settles the problem in favor of evolution.

to strain special foods out of the water. Nothing primitive or simple about these Cambrian creatures!

Now the big question is: *where are the ancestors of these Cambrian fossils?* We find no organisms with partially-formed intestines, stomachs, bristles, spines, appendages, eyes, feelers, and gills. Where are all the simpler creatures that should have led up to these complex forms — if total evolution is supposed to be a scientific fact? This problem is so acute that even Darwin himself admitted that it "may truly be urged as a valid argument" against evolution. Darwin hoped that more fossils would turn up these ancestors of the Cambrains, but a century later they are still missing. Some fossil remains occur in the Precambrian, it is true, but nothing that could possibly qualify as the ancestors of these Cambrian fossils. Most texts refer to this phenomenon as a "flowering" or an "explosion" of varied animal life in the Cambrian times.

Yet most books that describe this "Cambrian explosion" seem to miss the obvious implication of the phenomenon. They gloss over it as if it were no problem at all for evolution. For example, one popular text, *Matter, An Earth Science,* by Paul F. Brandwein, remarks that,

> There is an almost complete lack of distinct fossils in the Precambrian rocks. The absence of fossilized shells and the hard parts of animals is particularly surprising, since fossil evidence for animal life begins so abruptly in the Cambrian period. Also, the first abundant animal fossils are not simple, primitive forms, but somewhat advanced invertebrates.[25]

Evolutionists sometimes ask creationists: "Can you produce clear-cut evidence that clearly suggests creation? Can you point to something that can *only* be explained by creation?"

25. (New York: Harcourt, Brace, Jovanovich), p. 350. See also Marchall Kay and Edwin H. Colbert, *Stratigraphy and Life History* (New York: Wiley, 1965), pp. 102, 103.

Of course, this is an unfair demand, and would also destroy evolution, but I venture to suggest that a good sign of creation would be the appearance of something without antecedents. Doesn't the sudden explosion or flowering of these Cambrian animals with no apparent antecedents suggest creation rather than evolution? It's possible, I admit, that evolution has occurred and that for some strange reason the antecedents have disappeared. But the main point to remember is that the existing condition of the fossil rocks suggests creation, while the theory of evolution must, once again, *explain away* that condition, must suggest something that can't be observed. Sometimes it seems that the only reason one can give for the antecedents disappearing is that evolution requires it!

But there is more that is missing!

7. The Missing Transitional Forms

Similar to the mysterious missing Cambrian ancestors are the mysterious "missing links" that have troubled the theory of evolution ever since Darwin. These missing transitional forms in the rocks are also missing in animals that are alive today. In fact, the gaps in the fossil record correspond closely to the gaps we have between animal and plant groups today. Ever since Darwin scientists have been searching for these missing forms; they have become a kind of Holy Grail for the evolutionists.

For instance, nearly all new categories above the level of family (i.e. order, class, phylum) appear in the fossil record suddenly and are not led up to by gradually more complex forms, as you would expect. There is a big lacuna from protozoa to metazoa, from fish to amphibians, from amphibians to reptiles, from reptiles to birds and mammals, and from invertebrates to vertebrates. Creatures like the bat and the whale stand almost totally isolated in the stream of life, with no forms to connect them with the groups of their origin. If gills became lungs and fins became legs and scales became feathers then why is it that we find no transitional forms that combine features of both types of creatures?

Professor Simpson is usually quoted when this point about the missing links is made:

> In spite of these examples, it remains true, as every paleontologist knows, that *most* new species, genera, and families, and that nearly all categories above the level of families, appear in the record suddenly and are not led up to by known, gradual, completely continuous transitional sequences.[26]

Yet on the same page Simpson adds the remark that paleontologists "find it logical, if not scientifically required, to assume that the sudden appearance of a new systematic group is not evidence for creation." One could hardly ask for better proof of the essentially anti-religious bias of an evolutionist than this remark. Simpson says, in essence, "We know missing links are a problem for evolution, but we know they don't prove creation." It sounds like evolution is invincible, which is really having your cake and eating it too. What exactly in the scientific method demands that we not use creation to explain the missing links? Is this a way of saying that science is necessarily anti-theistic? It would seem so, on first reading.

In contrast to Simpson, we find this rather humble admission from Professor Stephen Jay Gould of Harvard:

> The extreme rarity of transitional forms in the fossil record persists as the trade secret of paleontology. . . . We fancy ourselves as the only true students of life's history, yet to

---

26. *Major Features of Evolution* (New York: Columbia University Press, 1953), p. 360. See also his *Tempo and Mode in Evolution* (New York: Columbia University Press, 1944), p. 106.

preserve our favored account of evolution by natural selection we view our data so bad that we never see the very process we profess to study.[27]

Evolutionists used to explain the missing transitional forms by pointing to the scarcity of fossil materials, but after a century of collecting fossils this reply sounds very lame. Heribert-Nilsson of Lund University, Sweden, says that after 40 years of study in paleontology and botany he was finally forced to conclude: "It is not even possible to make a caricature of an evolution out of paleobiological facts. The fossil material is now so complete that . . . the lack of transitional series cannot be explained as due to the scarcity of the material. The deficiencies are real; they will never be filled."[28]

If the gaps between animals are painful to evolution, those between the plants are even worse, says Professor E.J.H. Corner of Cambridge University. "Much evidence can be adduced in favor of the theory of evolution—from biology, biogeography, and paleontology, but I still think that to the unprejudiced the fossil record of plants is in favor of special creation."[29]

The problem of missing links has caused evolutionists to panic at times and rush to identify some dubious creature as a possible transitional form. Exhibit A for a long time was the *coelacanth,* a fish that supposedly had embryonic limbs on its fins, proving it was trying to turn into an amphibian. It was said to be extinct for millions of years, so it was a bit embarrassing to evolutionists when this fish was discovered in 1938 alive and kicking in the waters near Madagascar. It had kept its same structure for hundreds of millions of years!

---

27. "Evolution's Erratic Pace," *Natural History* (1977), 86 (5): 14.
28. *Synthetische Artbildung,* (1953), as cited in Morris, *Scientific Creationism,* p. 80.
29. Cited in Gish, *Evolution? The Fossils Say No!,* p. 116.

Another poor example of a missing link is *Archaeopteryx,* an ancient bird that seems to have some reptilian character- istics. Most ornithologists, however, classify it simply as a bird, since it possessed a beautiful, fully-formed set of feathers. Some of the reptilian features prove nothing in particular; teeth, for example, do not prove a creature kin to the rep- tiles since not all reptiles have teeth. Teeth are found in some birds, some fish, some amphibians, and some mam- mals also, but not in all of these groups. Hence, the possession of teeth proves nothing in particular. At most, *Archaeopteryx* is an organism that had characteristics similar to several kinds of organisms, just as the platypus has features similar to beavers, hairy mammals, and egg-laying animals.

At any rate, there surely must have been hundreds of thousands of transitional forms between *Archaeopteryx* and its putative reptile ancestor. Why can't we find a fossil with scales gradually becoming feathers? Or with forelimbs gradually turning into wings? Or with cold blood gradually turning into warm blood? Or with low metabolism gradually turning into high metabolism? Or with solid bone turning into airy bone? All these changes had to be accomplished between reptile and bird if evolution is true. Why no intermediate forms? To jump on a creature with a fully-formed set of wings and feathers is surely proof of the lack of evidence for a true link between reptile and bird.

How, then, should we explain this absence of intermediate forms in the fossil record? Many evolutionists say that transi- tional forms were so few and so unusual that they left no fossil remains. They argue that the origins of every group necessarily disappeared and it was only when a phylum had become well established that it began to leave any fossil remains. This sounds suspiciously like special pleading. It is a bit too convenient for the theory that all the transitional forms just disappeared.

A better explanation, I suggest, is that no intermediate or transitional forms ever existed. As John N. Moore concludes, "Just as there is no conclusive evidence from animal breeding or plant breeding records of the existence of fully fertile transitions or hybrids between major kinds of organisms, the same general condition exists as far as the fossil record is concerned."[30]

The situation here is similar to the problem faced by Psychoanalysis, another discipline that vaunts itself as scientific but lacks genuine proof. The key theory in Sigmund Freud's system of Psychoanalysis is the Oedipus Complex, which asserts that neuroses and psychoses arise from an inability to overcome sexual longings for the parent of the opposite sex. This complex requires a certain view of *infantile sexuality,* sexual fantasies occurring during the very earliest years of life.

As Dr. Martin Gross suggests in his *Psychological Society* (Random House, 1978), the temptation is strong to ask: Why can't we remember these first sexual desires? Freud answers, we repress it because we prefer to forget this forbidden, incestuous love. But this thesis of "infantile amnesia" is just a convenient way of avoiding proof for the alleged infantile sexuality. Modern research indicates that instead of forgetting our original childhood experiences, most of us never originally remembered them.

In like manner, the necessary disappearance of the transitional forms suggested by evolutionists seems to be just a convenient way of avoiding proof for the theory of evolution. We are told that the earth just "repressed" the missing links!

Once again, we note that creation predicts the very thing we find — missing links. Evolution does not predict them

---

30. *Questions and Answers on Creation/Evolution* (Grand Rapids, Michigan: Baker, 1976), p. 51.

and thus must struggle to explain them away. Any model that has to struggle to explain the facts so much will finally die.

8. The Phenomenon of Design in the Universe

The final feature of the universe we offer as evidence for the creation model is design. Perhaps we should say apparent design, since many thinkers will protest the assertion that the cosmos is clearly designed. The creationist argument at this point is obviously based on inference and probability; no theistic teleologist ever claims that he has found God directly and confirmed his existence. The evidence is indirect and inferential and thus a matter of faith, or loose science, not strict science. The Design (Teleological) Argument is one of the oldest and most popular proofs for God, and, for some strange reason, even its most energetic critics, Hume and Kant, expressed a certain respect for it.[31]

Materialists and mechanists sometimes ridicule the Design Argument by asserting that its mode of reasoning is anthropomorphic, mythological, and pre-scientific. In defense, we note that people, even scientists, use teleological explanations in several important areas of life.[32]

1. We use teleological reasoning when we infer the existence of other minds. We must use it, or else we have no right to believe that *persons* are anything more than mindless automata. You will never experience directly the operations of a person's mind, his emotions, plans, intentions, or purposes; you experience directly only the external behavior of other people.

---

31. See Hume's *Dialogues Concerning Natural Religion*, ed. Henry D. Aiken (New York: Hafner, 1948).

32. The following is adapted from my *Dear Agnos: A Defense of Christianity* (Grand Rapids, Michigan: Baker, 1976), pp. 73-75. Reprinted in 1980 under the title *The Case for Christian Apologetics*.

2. We use teleology in psychoanalysis. A good psychiatrist assumes that behind the aberrant behavior of his patient lies an unconscious purpose or drive or passion, a purpose that even the patient himself can't recognize or evaluate.

3. We use teleology when we interpret artifacts, especially those fashioned by people of ancient times. An archaeologist digging in a Stone Age site may come across a weapon that vaguely resembles a tomahawk, but only if the teleological principle is valid can he ascribe the tool to human ingenuity. In fact, one of the earliest known tools, the *eolith* (literally "dawn stone"), is very difficult to distinguish from a rock shaped by natural forces. Most people have such an instinctive use of teleology that they apply it unreflectively to human tools, no matter how crude.

4. It may sound strange, but in this case for design science may be our star witness! Why? Every time science advances our understanding of the universe, it adds a new link to the Design Argument chain-armor. Science assumes that there is a correspondence between the mind and the universe, between intelligence and nature. Our intellects can interpret nature and so nature must, in some sense, be intelligible. A totally absurd entity would resist intelligent interpretation. Just as the speech of a madman would be meaningless to a sane person, so also an absurd universe would defy rational analysis. Science couldn't "decode" or "read" or "translate" nature if natural events were just random occurrences exemplifying no general principles.

Immediately you may object: this sounds too anthropomorphic, it imposes an interpretation on nature that is all-too-human. True, but doesn't science do the same? Science assumes that nature is rational — but isn't *reason* a human faculty? We fashion laws by using mathematics — but isn't math based on deduction, which is a process of human thought? Science is just as anthropomorphic as the Design Argument, for in both cases human reason claims to find its own rational constitution mirrored in external reality. The only alternative to this view is to say that there is no real order in the world about us, but that we impose our own orderly thought upon a disorderly world. This alternative would destroy not only the Design Argument but also science.

A good theory, we have noted, not only explains the facts but also has heuristic fallout, that is, it opens up new areas of investigation that permit you to find new facts, which in turn tend to confirm the original theory. The teleological assumption not only unites and explains a vast body of data; it also leads to new discoveries in science. For example, some of our chemical elements were discovered by a man who assumed that all chemical elements were related to each other in a rational, coherent pattern of classification. In 1869, the Russian chemist, Dmitri Ivanovich Mendeleev, took the sixty-three elements then known to science and arranged them according to their similarities. By thus comparing the elements according to their affinities, he discovered that their properties were periodic functions of their atomic weights, that is, that their properties repeated themselves periodically after each seven elements.

Using this teleological hypothesis, Mendeleev was able to correct the previously-assigned atomic weights of certain elements. His corrections were upheld by later research. He also predicted rather brashly that the gaps in his classification system would someday be filled. He even predicted the new elements by name: eka-boron, eka-aluminum, and eka-silicon. All three were discovered in just a few years. If the ability to predict is the sign of a good theory, then the teleological hypothesis seems to be a good one.[33]

---

33. See Bernard Jaffe, *Crucibles: The Story of Chemistry from Ancient Alchemy to Nuclear Fission* (New York: Simon and Schuster, 1951), p. 208.

Now that we have defended the teleological mode of reasoning, let's look at the universe. Just about everywhere you turn you meet instances of natural law and order. In general, the universe seems amenable to rational analysis. The cosmos, moreover, seems basically friendly to life, mind, personality, and values. Our earth and solar system seem suspiciously contrived to bring about the appearance of these things. For example,

1. *The size of the earth is just right.* If it were much larger it would hold too many gases inimical to life, but if it were much smaller its gravitational forces could not have retained any atmosphere at all. Hence our earth has just sufficient mass to hold around itself a blanket of gases that both supports life and shields life from the lethal rays of the sun.

2. *The earth's rate of revolution is just right.* The rate of revolution makes it ideal for the continuous renewal of the atmosphere for animal life. The stability of carbon dioxide depends upon alternating light and darkness and hence the plants have just sufficient times of light and darkness to regenerate the air.

3. *The earth's distance from the sun is just right.* All living tissue is made of chains of carbon molecules whose characteristics are retained only within a narrow range of temperature. If we were closer to the sun or farther away it would be either too hot or too cold to maintain such tissue.

4. *The earth's seasons are just right.* Seasonal variations, caused by the 23° tilt of the earth's axis, are vital for human life. If certain conditions did not vary then some very harmful microorganisms would multiply beyond all control and destroy the human race. The variation of seasons controls such harmful microorganisms.

5. *The land-water ratio is just right.* The ratio of water to land is about 3 to 1. If we had more water the land area would be like a swamp; if we had more land it would be like a desert. As it is, the ratio produces sufficient rainfall to grow plants on the land.

6. *The earth's satellite is vital.* Our moon is the largest known satellite relative to the size of its parent body. Hence, the moon has sufficient mass to cause tides and tides are very helpful in keeping the oceans fresh. Tides "flush" the oceans and vitalize them, just as currents vitalize a river.

If these large features of earth and life don't impress you, then look at the evidence for design in one of the smallest places — the amazing DNA molecule, the tiny unit of life that carries the genetic code for all living things. The problem of how such a complex molecule could be the result of random action is greatly increased by the fact that the DNA molecule can neither be reproduced nor its messages translated without precise enzymes, and that the production of these enzymes in turn is exactly controlled by the DNA. This is a closed cirlce: the DNA won't work without the enzymes and the enzymes can't be produced without the DNA. But which came first? In *American Scientist* (59:305), Caryl P. Haskins asks the inevitable question:

> Did the code and the means of translating it appear simultaneously in evolution? It seems almost incredible that any such coincidence could have occurred, given the extraordinary complexities of both sides and the requirement that they be coordinated accurately for survival. By a pre-Darwinian (or a skeptic of evolution after Darwin) this puzzle would surely have been interpreted as the most powerful sort of evidence for special creation.

This is just a small list of the features of our world that support the Design Argument.[34] There seems to be a conspiracy

---

34. For more material, see the following works: Arthur C. Custance *Evolution or Creation?* Vol. IV, "The Doorway Papers," (Grand Rapids, Michigan: Zondervan, 1976), pp. 28-31; L. J. Henderson, *The Fitness of the Environment* (New York: Macmillan, 1913); *The Order of Nature* (Cambridge, Mass.: Harvard University Press, 1917); A. Cressy Morrison, *Man Does Not Stand Alone* (Old Tappan, N.J.: Revell, 1944); Lecomte du Nouy, *Human Destiny* (New York: David McKay, 1947); William Paley, *Natural Theology,* ed. F. Ferré (New York: Library of Liberal Arts, 1962).

among the elements to produce life, mind, and values, a conspiracy so strong that two evolutionists could write a book called *Biochemical Predestination*! Now, as R. J. Nogar says, "Contrary and discordant things cannot, always or in the most cases, be parts of one order except under someone's government."[35] He gives the example of the arrow:

> An arrow shot into the air is subject to many contrary and discordant processes: gravity, air pressure, wind, etc. When several arrows reach the center of the target, thus ruling out the possibility of mere chance, one must say that this was the result of an expert archer.[36]

We close this argument for design and for creation with a noteworthy confession from P.A.M. Dirac, one of the world's foremost mathematical physicists:

> It seems to be one of the fundamental features of nature that fundamental physical laws are described in terms of a mathematical theory of great beauty and power, needing quite a high standard of mathematics for one to understand it. You may wonder: why is nature constructed along these lines? One can only answer that our present knowledge seems to show that nature is so constructed. We simply have to accept it. One could perhaps describe the situation by saying that God is a mathematician of a very high order, and He used very advanced mathematics in constructing the universe. Our feeble attempts at mathematics enable us to understand a bit of the universe, as we proceed to develop higher and higher mathematics we can hope to understand the universe better.[37]

If our reasoning thus far is correct, the creation model is a viable model for origins, better perhaps, than evolution.

---

35. *The Wisdom of Evolution* (New York: Doubleday, 1963), p. 310. Nogar is a theistic evolutionist.

36. *Ibid.,* p. 311.

37. "The Evolution of the Physicist's Picture of Nature," *Scientific American,* Vol. 208 (May, 1963), p. 53.

WHAT IF EVOLUTION WERE TRUE?

Let us summarize the results of this chapter by listing the features of the universe that creation explains better than evolution, features that are predictions of creation but problems for evolution.

1. If evolution were true, you would find laws of nature or the structure of reality gradually changing and developing. You don't. Things seem very stable at this time.

2. If evolution were true, you would find a law of innovation, a tendency of increasing order. You don't. You find a conservation of matter/energy (First Law of Thermodynamics) and a rule of disorder, an increase of entropy, a dissipation of energy (Second Law of Thermodynamics).

3. If evolution were true, you would find a gradual record in the rocks of increasingly complex life forms. You don't. You find a sudden explosion or flowering of complex forms in the Cambrian rocks.

4. If evolution were true, you would find intermediate forms between the major groups of animals. You don't. You find puzzling gaps, with very few, if any, genuine transitional forms.

5. If evolution were true, you would find more beneficial mutations to provide an effective mechanism for evolution. You don't. You find 99% of them either neutral or harmful. You find capable geneticists like Goldschmidt and Gould seriously toying with "hopeful monsters" to provide a mechanism.

Now, even with all these difficulties, I admit that evolution could possibly be true. But if it is, its truth certainly isn't apparent and its proof isn't demonstrative. Frankly, it is hurting for evidence. If you went into court with evidence like this the jury would surely rule, "Not guilty." Such problems as these would at least make a cautious man suspend judgment on the question of origins.

And . . . such problems should certainly make us stop the policy of teaching only evolution in the public schools.

4

OBJECTIONS TO TEACHING CREATION

If our reasoning up to this point has been sound, we must conclude that creation is a viable model of origins. If the problem of origins is still an open question, and if creation is one of the two possible options, you would expect it to be investigated in the public schools when origins is discussed.

But it isn't. Why?

Evolutionists give a number of reasons for legitimately excluding creation from the public schools, especially from the science classes. In this chapter we will examine some of the most important objections.

Before we analyze objections, we should keep in mind that it is not necessary for the creationist to completely destroy evolution or completely establish creation in order to make a case for equal treatment of creation. Both should be examined because origins is an open question and these seem to be the only choices. But for the evolutionist to maintain his practice of teaching only evolution you would expect some decisive proof of the theory or some blockbuster objection to teaching creation.

In my judgment, the evolutionist has neither.

EVOLUTION HAS BEEN PROVED

Some evolutionists contend that we shouldn't teach creation because evolution has been proved and has eliminated creation. Carl Sagan claims that the fossil record and modern molecular biology have demonstrated evolution. G. G. Simpson insists that "evolution must be considered not only as a theory but, in a correct vernacular sense, as an established fact," and he adds, "to teach otherwise would be to try to set history back to the Middle Ages."[1]

This assertion gets us into a briar patch of scientific methodology and scientific philosophy. When exactly does a theory become a fact? Does some board rule on this matter? Is there a Pope of Science or an Archbishop of Evolution to hand down an *ex cathedra* pronouncement? Sagan and Simpson seem to be a bit credulous, because many other scientists contend that evolution has not yet been proved and is still in the realm of hypothesis. These men are not creationists, as you might expect, but simply scientists who are interested in the problem of scientific truth in general and anxious to keep scientific standards at a high level.

For example, Paul Ehrlich and L. C. Birch make this candid confession:

Our theory of evolution has become . . . one which cannot be refuted by any possible observations. Every conceivable

---

1. Letter from Simpson, "To Whom It May Concern," Tucson, Arizona, August 1, 1972. This letter was written to support the position of Professor G. Ledyard Stebbins of the University of California, Davis, on the problem of the missing transitional forms.

observation can be fitted into it. It is thus "outside of empirical science," but not necessarily false. No one can think of ways in which to test it. Ideas, either without basis or based on a few laboratory experiments carried out in extremely simplified systems, have attained currency far beyond their validity. They have become part of *an evolutionary dogma* accepted by most of us as part of our training.[2]

In discussing the various historical attempts to prove evolution by experimentation, Loren Eiseley notes that,

With the failure of these many efforts, science was left in the somewhat embarrassing position of having to postulate theories of living origins which it could not demonstrate. After having chided the theologian for his reliance on myth and miracle, science found itself in the unenviable position of having to create a mythology of its own, namely, the assumption that what, after long effort could not be proved to take place today had, in truth, taken place in the primeval past.[3]

N. J. Berril, while tracing out the origins of the vertebrates, admits that,

There is no direct proof or evidence that any of the suggested events or changes ever took place; what strength the argument may have comes from whatever wealth of circumstantial detail I have been able to muster. In a sense, this account is science fiction, but I have myself found it an interesting and enjoyable venture to speculate concerning the Cambrian and Pre-Cambrian happenings that may have led to my own existence.[4]

In his introduction to the 1956 edition of Darwin's *Origin of Species,* W. R. Thompson speaks critically of those who would thrust evolution prematurely into the circle of fact:

2. *Nature,* Vol. 214 (1967), p. 353. Italics are mine.
3. *The Immense Journey* (New York: Random House, 1957), p. 199.
4. *The Origin of Vertebrates* (Oxford University Press, 1955), p. 10.

I am not satisfied that Darwin proved his point or that his influence in scientific and public thinking has been beneficial. . . . There is a great divergence of opinion among biologists, not only about the causes of evolution but even about the actual process. This divergence exists because the evidence is unsatisfactory and does not permit any certain conclusion. It is, therefore, right and proper to draw the attention of the non-scientific public to the disagreements about evolution. But some recent remarks of evolutionists show that they think this is unreasonable. This situation, where scientific men rally to the defense of a doctrine they are unable to define scientifically, much less demonstrate with scientific rigor, attempting to maintain its credit with the public by the suppression of criticism and the elimination of difficulties, is abnormal and undesirable in science.[5]

M. T. Ghiselin warns us to take account of the speculative nature of much evolutionary thinking:

It is true that many works on phylogeny do read like imaginative literature rather than science. A disproportionate segment of the literature seeks to fill gaps in the data with speculations and nothing more.[6]

R. H. Peters feels that evolution lacks the crucial attribute of empirical testability:

I argue that the "theory of evolution" does not make predictions, so far as ecology is concerned, but is instead a logical formula which can be used only to classify empiricisms, and to show the relationships which such a classification implies. . . . These theories are actually tautologies and, as such, cannot make empirically testable predictions. *They are not scientific theories at all.*[7]

---

5. (London, J. M. Dent and Son, 1956), pp. 5, 17.

6. "Models of Phylogeny," in *Models in Paleobiology,* edited by T. J. M. Schopf (San Francisco: Freeman Cooper, 1972).

7. "Tautology in Evolution and Ecology," *American Naturalist,* Vol. 110, No. 1 (1976), p. 1. Tom Bethell also argues that the theory of Darwinism is a tautology and thus empirically sterile, in his article, "Darwin's Mistake," *Harper's Magazine,* February, 1976, p. 75.

If Ehrlich, Birch, Eiseley, Berril, Thompson, Ghiselin, and Peters are correct, then evolution has not advanced much beyond its status in 1859. Even Darwin admitted in 1860 to Herbert Spencer that "of my numerous (private) critics, you are almost the only one who has put the philosophy of the argument, as it seems to me, in a fair way — namely, as an hypothesis (with some innate probability) . . . which explains several groups of facts."[8]

No doubt one major reason some scientists are willing to believe that evolution has been proved is that it explains much of the data one can assemble. But we must repeat that sometimes more than one hypothesis can account for the same facts. As we noted in the last chapter, you commit the fallacy of Asserting the Consequent when you accept a theory just because it explains the facts.

For example, one of the most frequent proofs for evolution is the similarity of animal forms. Comparative anatomy, it is urged, proves that similar animals had a common ancestry. One can easily see an analogy between nails and hoofs, hands and claws, fish scales and bird feathers. There is certainly a striking similarity between a bat's wing, a man's arm, and a whale's flipper. We are almost persuaded to be evolutionists until someone poses the simple question: does structural similarity *demand* genetic relationship? Is Evolution the only possible explanation of similarity?

No. Structural similarity could be a predictable result of either creation or evolution. How do you know for sure that a Creator-Designer wouldn't also come up with similar structures? Since the laws of motion, aerodynamics, and hydrodynamics are the same all over the earth, wouldn't

---

8. *Life and Letters of Herbert Spencer,* edited by David Duncan, I, 128.

it be reasonable to suppose that a Designer would make wings that resemble arms, scales that resemble feathers, arms that resemble flippers, and nails that resemble hoofs?

Take an analogy from human creation: a ship, a bridge, and an office building resemble each other because they all have steel girders, but this doesn't prove they have a genetic relationship. It could just as well prove that they all were made by the same architect, who, in all three cases, needed a certain structure for a certain function.

The weakness of this argument from similarity was clearly perceived by a certain biology student who observed: "They find a muscle in an animal and they give it a name. Then they find a similar muscle in a similar animal and give it the same name and then exclaim, 'Hey, look! Evolution!'"

Hence, comparative anatomy — and this goes for all kinds of proof based on similarity — fails to confirm the theory of evolution because the predicted result could be true of creation also. What we need is some datum that will decisively confirm or disconfirm one theory or the other. We need a datum or data that could *only* be explained by creation or evolution. As Karl Popper reminds us, it is much easier to falsify an incorrect theory than to verify a correct theory.[9]

Sometimes evolutionists try to win this battle by default, by saying that creation is impossible. British scientist Sir Arthur Keith asserted that evolution was unproved and unprovable but that scientists still held to it because the only possible alternative, creation, was incredible. This is a logical fallacy called *Argumentum ad Ignorantiam,* "an argument addressed to ignorance." You commit this fallacy when you reason that since one position can't prove itself the other wins by default. This is an error for two reasons:

---

9. *Conjectures and Refutations* (New York: Basic Books, 1963), pp. 114-115.

(1) First, before you can win by default, you must prove that there are only two possible theories. There may be a third or a fourth possibility. It would be silly for one combatant to shout, "I win!," when he has eliminated only one alternative theory and others are waiting to enter the contest.

But, you object, haven't we already admitted that there are only two theories on this matter of origins? Wouldn't the failure to establish creation prove evolution?

(2) No, because even if I grant that we have only two theories, the failure to prove one doesn't prove the other, *unless* you have some *independent* evidence to support the second theory. If creation isn't proved — we allow this only to make the point — then it might be that we should just suspend judgment, not opt for evolution. The most you can conclude is that, at present, we have insufficient data for making a scientific judgment.

For example, there is either life on Mars or there is none. So far, we haven't found any life on Mars. Should we conclude, then, that there is no life on Mars? No, because there could still be life on Mars and we just haven't discovered it yet. To argue otherwise would be fallacious.

Norman Macbeth reports that he finds this fallacy very prevalent among scientists (he is a jurist). He points out that when a man propounds a theory he is obligated to support every link in the chain of his reasoning, while a critic or skeptic may peck away at any aspect of the theory, testing it for flaws. A critic isn't obligated to set up any theory of his own or offer any alternate theory; he can be purely negative if he wants to. "If a theory conflicts with the facts or with reason," concludes Macbeth, "it is entitled to no respect. . . . Whether a better theory is offered, is irrelevant."[10]

---

10. *Darwin Retried — An Appeal to Reason* (Boston: Gambit, 1971), pp. 5-7.

Even if evolution hasn't been adequately proved, most scientists in the world believe in it and this brings us to the second objection.

MOST SCIENTISTS BELIEVE IN EVOLUTION

If most scientists believe in evolution, then it must be the only theory that deserves the mantle of science and, consequently, the only one we should teach in school. This argument sways a lot of people, but it, too, is based on a recognized logical error, the fallacy called Misuse of Authority.

There is certainly nothing wrong in citing a competent authority to support your position — if you don't break certain rules. Misuse of Authority occurs when you break two basic rules about using testimony from experts.

(1) First, you must be careful using an expert to prove something unrelated to his field of competence. An expert on Renaissance art is not equipped to help you with your nutrition problems. No man can be an expert on every topic. Some men are world authorities in a limited field and faddists in other fields. Some Nobel Prize winners prove to be poorly informed in fields outside of their specialization.

Yet evolutionists think that all they have to do to prove evolution is to parrot the old cliché, "Most scientists believe in evolution." In the first place, most of the scientists mentioned in the assertion aren't even in the fields related to evolution. Many of them — like engineers, chemists, and astronomers — wouldn't even know how to begin an argument for evolution. They accept it because those "in the club," who are supposed to know, hold to evolution.

In the second place, the assertion may be false, or at least exaggerated. *Many scientists believe in creation.* "Most" can mean anything from 50.1% to 99.9% and we have no way of knowing where the "most" falls. Even if you could determine that over 50.1% of scientists believe in evolution it wouldn't prove anything to a careful thinker. Is anyone seriously suggesting that a poll of scientists is a valid criterion for scientific truth? That would be the Gallup-Harris method, not the scientific method. As far as I can determine, counting noses has no place in the scientific method.

Ask yourself: "Has there ever been a time in the history of science when a widely-held position was given up by scientists?" Yes, most certainly. One obvious case would be the last century when most scientists before Darwin held to creation and then changed to evolution. You could easily have argued in the year 1860 that, "Most scientists believe in creation, so evolution must be wrong."

An intellectual historian could cite many more examples of this phenomenon, e.g.

a. What could you prove with a poll of scientists from Nazi Germany's Third Reich on the question of race?

b. What could you prove from a poll of physicists on the question of ether before the twentieth century?

c. What could you prove from a poll of learned men in the Middle Ages on the shape of the earth?

d. A classic example is the case of T. D. Lysenko in Russia. In the 1930's and 40's Lysenko, with Stalin backing him, got control of the Academy of Agricultural Science and the Institute of Genetics. The problem was that Lysenko insisted that all Russian geneticists teach Lamarkism, the doctrine of inheritance of acquired characteristics, a mechanism for evolution which, presumably, was more in harmony with Marxism than the idea of mutational selection. Lysenko brutalized and tyrannized his opponenets, many of whom were arrested and died in concentration camps. Soviet genetics was the laughing stock of the world for two decades.

Only in 1956 was Lysenko removed. What would a poll of Russian scientists have proved during his regime?

We could list examples like this for several pages, but the point is simply that one should be careful not to deify the current opinion on anything. For sundry reasons learned men have held to certain theories in the past that turned out to be false.

(2) But an even subtler misuse of authority occurs when you cite an expert on an issue — even in his field — and then you assume that his evaluation is infallible. Don't forget that your expert is still human, finite, and subject to error. Piltdown Man fooled the experts for decades. Many experts can amass a mountain of facts on a certain topic but fail to relate the facts properly, or fail to draw the proper inferences from them. Sometimes a high school student can detect an error in inference made by an expert. The great Einstein divided by zero at one point in his relativity calculations — a schoolboy mistake that was detected by a Russian mathematician, Alexander Friedmann.

So the upshot of this argument from scientific consenus is that we should ask not, "What do the scientists believe?" but rather, "What is the evidence?" If all those beautiful people believe in evolution then there must be some good, decisive evidence for it. Give us the evidence, not the poll, because your poll is irrelevant. But, as we have seen, the decisive evidence for evolution is lacking.

Why, then, do scientists still believe in evolution? The intellectual historian can tell you that many times in world history most people, even most learned people, have held to a belief which later turned out to be unfounded, not because the evidence was overwhelming, but because of some social or psychological need to believe it. You might call it the "tyranny of the Zeitgeist." As V. F. Calverton observes, we sometimes have a "cultural compulsive" that makes us hold to certain doctrines, beliefs that we never even examine. When Darwin first propounded evolution, "every force in the environment, economic and social, conspired to the success of the doctrine" of natural selection and the survival of the fittest.[11] As George Bernard Shaw said, people "jumped at Darwin."

E. G. Boring points out that scientists, like all people, will cling tenaciously to conceptual schemes even in the light of mounting evidence against them. They form an emotional attachment to hypotheses and theories they have come to accept. There is a pride of authorship, a fierce loyalty to the conceptual scheme which the individual has espoused.[12]

Further, once a theory is accepted by the majority of intellectuals, with or without evidence, it can become a tyrannical paradigm, a cultural myth that grinds all its opponents into the dust. It builds an army called peer pressure to protect it. Dr. Thomas Dwight, Parkmann Professor of Anatomy at Harvard, made this remarkable confession in 1927:

> The tyranny of the *Zeitgeist* in the matter of evolution is overwhelming to a degree of which outsiders have no idea; not only does it influence (as I must admit that it does in my own case) our manner of thinking, but there is the oppression as in the days of the "terror." How very few of the leaders of science dare tell the truth concerning their own state of mind! How many feel themselves forced in public to do a lip service to a cult they do not believe in! As Professor T. H. Morgan intimates, it is only too true that many of these who would on no account be guilty of an act which they recognize as dishonest, nevertheless speak and write habitually as if evolution were an absolute certainty as well established as the law of gravitation.[13]

11. *The Making of Man* (New York: Modern Library, 1931), p. 27.
12. *Science* (1964), 145:680-85.
13. *Thoughts of a Catholic Anatomist* (London: Longmans, Green, and Co., 1927), pp. 20, 21.

It proves nothing, therefore, that the majority of scientists believe in evolution. Misuse of Authority is used in TV commercials all the time but you really wouldn't expect it from the mouths of so many trained scientists.

EVOLUTION IS THE GREAT UNIFYING THEME OF BIOLOGY

Evolutionists argue that we must teach evolution because it is the great unifying theme of all biology, that without it the science would collapse into a heap of unorganized facts. Dr. G. L. Stebbins insists that, "The only sound way to teach biology as a scientific discipline in the contemporary modern world is to emphasize evolution as a basic explanation of origins."[14]

Anyone who affirms that evolution unifies the facts has a firm grasp of the obvious. Evolution unifies the fact of biology, up to a point, but then, so does creation, up to a point! The phrase "unifying theme" is just a synonym for theory, hypothesis, or model. Theories unify data; in fact, that is their function; if they don't unify data they are poor theories. To talk about evolution being "the great unifying theme of biology" is just a fancy way of saying that evolution is the theory currently held by most of the scientific community to explain biological data.

But all this is irrelevant. The relevant question is, as always, *what is the evidence for the theory*? Is that evidence conclusive? Is there decisive proof to establish evolution and eliminate creation? The answer, once again, is no.

---

14. "Evolution as the Central Theme of Biology," *A Compendium of Information on the Theory of Evolution and the Evolution-Creationism Controversy* (11250 Roger Bacon Drive, Reston, Virginia, 22090: National Association of Biology Teachers), p. 68.

L. Harrison Matthews admits that, "The fact of evolution is the backbone of biology," but then he adds, "biology is thus in the peculiar position of being a science founded on an unproved theory — is it then a science or a faith?" Matthews answers his own question: "Belief in the theory of evolution is thus exactly parallel to belief in creation — both are concepts which believers know to be true but neither, up to the present, has been capable of proof."[15]

The simple fact is, we can't let an unproved, unverified theory be taught as fact just because it satisfies someone's sense of symmetry. This is not only a defective methodology, it is also a dangerous intellectual practice. In his dialogue, *Phaedo,* Plato explained his epistemological approach in this way: "This is the method I adopted: I first assumed some principle which I judged to be the strongest, and then I affirmed as true whatever seemed to agree with it. . . . And that which disagreed I regarded as untrue."

Many evolutionists reason like Plato, that is, they adopt the criterion of Coherence and then they apply it uncritically. They claim as proved many things which really do not meet good experimental standards. This is why Erhlich and Birch could complain that "our theory of evolution has become . . . one which cannot be refuted by any possible observations. Every conceivable observation can be fitted into it. It is thus 'outside of empirical science.'"[16]

An uncritical use of the Coherence Method explains how frauds like Piltdown Man and Nebraska Man could be accepted by the scientific community, even by the experts in the matter, and go for decades undetected. The fraud fitted the paradigm, so no one examined it carefully. It was

---

15. See his Introduction to Darwin's *Origin of Species* (London: J. M. Dent and Sons, 1971), pp. x, xi.

16. *Nature,* Vol. 214 (1967), p. 353.

"just what the doctor ordered." The fraud was exposed only when some scientists were true to their best methodology and insisted on the good old rule: *paradigms must be constantly tested against the facts.*

Perhaps we can learn from another discipline: history. Practicing historians are usually rather wary of grandiloquent, metahistorical systems, such as those propounded by Arnold Toynbee, Oswald Spengler, and Teilhard de Chardin. They find such complex schemes difficult to check and verify. You would never find a history department teaching Toynbee, Spengler, and Chardin as fact. More likely you would find them treated in a course called, "Philosophy of History," or "Theories of History," just as the problem of personality is often taught by psychology departments in courses called, "Theories of Personality."

Practicing historians feel that the historian should be very cautious when speculating about the final, ultimate meaning of history, because that lies partly in the realm of faith and metahistory. H. A. L. Fisher writes:

> One intellectual excitement has . . . been denied me. Men wiser and more learned than I have discerned in history a plot, a rhythm, a predetermined pattern. These harmonies are concealed from me. I can see only one emergency following upon another as wave follows wave, only one great fact with respect to which, *since it is unique, there can be no generalization,* only one safe rule for the historian: that he should recognize . . . the play of the contingent and the unforeseen.[17]

If Toynbee should argue like Stebbins and insist that his theory of history is the great unifying theme of all history and that without it history would collapse into a pile of

---

17. *History of Europe,* Vol. I, p. vii, cited in *Science, Faith, and Man: European Thought since 1914,* edited by W. Warren Wagar (New York: Harper, 1968), p. 260.

atomistic fact units, Fisher would probably reply that unity or coherence is not the only criterion for a good theory. A good theory must be testable in experience or else it remains just a possible model. Better to have no unifying theme than to have an unverified one.

I say the same to the evolutionist!

TEACHING CREATION PLACES UNNECESSARY STRESS ON THE TEACHER

Dr. William V. Mayer, director of the Biological Sciences Curriculum Study, points out that "the training of teachers does not prepare them for the presentation of theological materials."[18] Teaching creation, therefore, would place an unusual burden on the shoulders of the public school science teachers. Dr. Mayer further complains that science instructors would be compelled to teach a narrow, fundamentalist view of Biblical creation.

First, let me say that I think it would be wrong to teach the strict Biblical version of creation in the public schools. Not only would you run afoul of the church-state separation (see the next objection), but you would also fail to represent fairly all those who believe in a general doctrine of creation but are not Jews or Christians. Men like Thomas Jefferson and Benjamin Franklin, for example, were strong believers in creation but both were deists and shunned association with any organized religion. Creation as a general cosmology, scientific creationism, if you please, is what we want presented in the public schools.

Second, as for Dr. Mayer's complaint that teachers are not trained to present theological materials, this is a tricky use of the word "theological" which conjures up lectures on

18. *Liberty,* Vol. 73, No. 5 (September-October, 1978), p. 6.

predestination, purgatory, and eschatology. Nothing like this will be necessary to teach creation. We train teachers to present whatever needs to be presented, whatever society, the family, or the local school board have decided should be passed on to posterity. To call creation theological is to confuse the issue as to whether creation is a viable model of origins or not. If science teachers can't teach creation then maybe origins ought to be avoided altogether in science classes. If both creation and evolution are viable theories of origins then teachers should be trained in the presentation of both.

My teachers taught me Marxism in my history classes — even though I was a Christian. They taught me Marxism in the sense that they explained what Marxists believed and why they believed it. My colleagues in history would smile if I now told them that I couldn't teach my Nineteenth Century Europe class because, being a Christian, I don't hold to Marxism!

What did we do when the New Math was introduced into the public schools? Did we forbear because the poor math teachers didn't understand it and hadn't been trained in it? No, we forced the poor math teachers to learn how to teach it. We made them attend special classes, night classes, summer school classes, seminars, workshops. When we judge something important we don't let the poor teachers keep us from doing it, do we?

Actually, teaching creation won't be all that difficult for any science teacher. Both models use the same data; they just explain them differently. To teach creation you just give the counterpart of evolution. Textbooks have already appeared that arrange the two models and what they teach in appropriate parallel columns.

One evolutionist asked me, "What will you *show* the students when you teach them creation?" I replied, "The same thing you show them to prove that birds came from reptiles — nothing!" When you're dealing with a theory you needn't *show* all the parts of the theory. If you could show everything then you wouldn't need a theory. Those cute little charts depicting the trees of life and the evolution from apes up to man are all based on nothing you can show; they are theoretical reconstructions. Neither model can show what it claims and we shouldn't demand it.

Yes, the poor teacher is always in our thoghts, but uppermost in our thoughts is justice. The student has the academic right to hear the other model of origins.

TEACHING CREATION IN THE
PUBLIC SCHOOLS IS ILLEGAL

Evolutionists argue that teaching creation in the public schools would violate the First Amendment to the United States Constitution, which reads, "Congress shall make no law respecting an establishment of religion, or prohibiting the free exercise thereof." This argument implies that teaching creation would violate the separation of church and state and would tend to favor one religion over another. This objection calls forth several observations in rebuttal.

First, let us ask, what if the situation were reversed and it was illegal to teach evolution? What would the evolutionists do? You know very well — they would complain loudly that that was a bad law, wouldn't they? Well, we creationists are just doing the same thing. If — I say *if* — it indeed is illegal to teach creation then we must insist that that is an unfair law.

Second, suppose that I could show that the General Theory of Evolution was taught in essence by some world religions?

63

(I can, by the way; see the next objection.) Would the evolutionist then wish to take it out of the classroom? No, he would argue, that regardless of its occurrence in a religious system or religious document it is also a scientific theory. He warms to his case by comparing it to a religious cult that breast-fed its babies because Zeus commanded it. Then science comes along and confirms by good laboratory proof that mother's milk is really the best. The superiority of breast feeding can thus be taught in school regardless of the fact that Zeus long ago commanded it.

That's fine, but the creationist argues the same way. Creation is a scientific theory — a legitimate explanation of the same facts that evolution tries to explain. Hence, we teach it because it is scientific, notwithstanding its occurrence in a religious document.

But more to the point, if we ask what was the original intent of the Founding Fathers in writing the First Amendment, the answer would be that they wanted to avoid a State Church, such as the Anglican Church in Great Britain or the Lutheran Church in Germany. But teaching creation as a model of origins could hardly result in the establishment of a State Church. Jefferson and Franklin both believed in creation but were not "churched."

It is really doubtful if our Founding Fathers were intending to give a commentary on the scientific method when they wrote the First Amendment. The argument that teaching creation violates the First Amendment assumes that the creators of the American republic favored a species of scientism, an exclusively empirical process of verification, which, if true, would destroy most of their own political accomplishments. You can't prove democracy or the dignity of man in the laboratory.

Wendell R. Bird puts the shoe on the other foot and charges that teaching only evolution violates the free exercise clause of the First Amendment. In a very learned article, which won the Egger Prize, Bird skillfully argues that teaching evolution as the only theory of origins violates the right of free exercise of religion by teaching materials that contradict the religious convictions of many students.[19]

Let's put a shoe on the evolutionist's other foot and argue that teaching evolution is illegal because it amounts to teaching a religion. Our argument has four steps:

1. The Supreme Court has defined Humanism as a religion.
2. Humanism teaches that the universe operates automatically and mechanistically, with no God affecting the process.
3. When you teach General Evolution you also teach that the universe operates automatically and mechanistically, with no God affecting the process.
4. Therefore, when you teach General Evolution you teach Humanism, a religion, in the public schools.

If we can prove statements 1, 2, and 3, then statement 4, the conclusion, follows necessarily. The proof is as follows:

1. In *Torcaso v. Watkins,* (1961) the Supreme Court mentions "Secular Humanism" as one example of "religions in this country which do not teach what would generally be considered a belief in the existence of God." Other examples given are Buddhism, Taoism, and Ethical Culture.

The Court was obviously correct in this designation. Humanism is a religion because it has a definite worldview, a metaphysics, cosmology, epistemology, and axiology. It teaches dedication to the human race and calls on its devotees to cultivate a religious-like devotion to these ideals. If you

---

19. "Freedom of Religion and Science Instruction in Public Schools," *The Yale Law Journal,* Vol. 87, No. 3 (January, 1978), pp. 515-570.

deny this because humanism has no god, then you would also have to reject as religious such systems as Taoism and Buddhism, which are always considered as religions.

2. The fact that Humanism has no god creating and preserving the universe needs little documentation. Humanists are very emphatic about the non-theistic teaching of their philosophy. If there is no eternal God to originate the universe and preserve it in its operations, it follows that eternal matter must have done it all.[20]

3. A conflict may occur here when we assert that General Evolution teaches the same thing as Humanism. Notice we didn't say simply evolution but "General Evolution," or Macroevolution, the doctrine that says evolution is total, from everlasting to everlasting. We are not referring to Special Evolution or microevolution, which is just a fancy term for mutation, speciation, or variation.

General Evolution says that matter, eternally in process, by some accident produces life, then from the struggle for existence come higher forms of life, then conscious life, then self-conscious life (man) . . . and it all happens automatically, without a plan or a planner. Simpson says that, "Man is the result of a purposeless and materialistic process that did not have him in mind. He was not planned. He is a state of matter, a form of life, a sort of animal."[21]

If Humanism is legally a religion, and if both Humanism and General Evolution teach a naturalistic, mechanistic universe, and if General Evolution is taught as fact in the public schools, it follows necessarily that Humanism is being taught as fact in our public schools. The only reason this blatant illegality could go on is that evolutionists have exploited the ambiguity of the terms "science" and "religion."

20. See Sir Julian Huxley's *The Humanist Frame* (New York: Harper, 1961), pp. 38-48.
21. *The Meaning of Evolution* (New Haven: Yale University Press, 1952), p. 344.

THERE ARE MANY THEORIES OF CREATION

Many evolutionists ask, "Which theory of creation should we teach?" There seem to be many — the Biblical, the Babylonian, Hindu, Buddhist, Nordic, Eskimo, Polynesian, and so on. If the poor teacher has to cover all these possible theories he will consume all his time in origins alone.

This sounds like a good objection, until you examine that basic assumption that there are several creation theories. Here we meet an old problem called "selective perception." You see what you want to see. If you insist on seeing many different theories of creation, then to you there are many. But if you will look underneath all the particulars and abstract the essence you will see that creation accounts fall into two types, one of which turns out, after analysis, to be just evolution in disguise. Like the word science, the word creation is sometimes used very loosely.

A genuine creation theory affirms the total production of being or reality by a personal God who is *prior* to the physical universe. Unless God comes before the material cosmos you have matter more ultimate than God, which means that God comes from matter, which turns out to be an absurd use of the word "God." Any theory which essentially affirms that God is prior to matter is a true creation model and deserves presentation in the public schools. If any non-Biblical theory of creation asserts this (not many do) it is very similar to the Hebrew-Christian account of creation. It may differ in details of the actual creation but if it asserts an everlasting Person or Mind who is the ultimate principle of explanation for the universe, it is a genuine creation model. The key is eternal God, as opposed to eternal matter.[22]

---

22. How could matter be eternal if it is running down, according to the Second Law of Thermodynamics? Can a decomposing entity be everlasting?

Now, as a matter of fact, most non-Biblical, mythological creation stories are already faithfully represented in the schools by the evolution model! I know that may sound surprising to most evolutionists — I was surprised when I first realized it — but it is true nonetheless. Nearly all non-Biblical creation accounts have the physical universe coming first and the god(s) arising later, out of the material substance. Matter is prior to the gods and matter develops, by magic, it seems, into all forms of being that we know.

One of the most primitive, primordial, and seminal creation myths is the ancient Babylonian epic, *Enuma Elish*.[23] Those who think that the Hebrews borrowed their creation story wholesale from the Babylonians need to note some critical differences in the two accounts:

1. Genesis has an everlasting God bring the temporal world into being. *Enuma Elish* has the everlasting elements — specifically water — coming before all the gods.[24]

2. Genesis has no theo-biography, no notion of the birth or development of God. In Babylon, the first supernal beings were demons and monsters who arise out of the water, while the great Marduk is born fairly late in the theogonic process.

3. Genesis proclaims the absolute subordination of the cosmos to God, the total control of creation by God. *Enuma Elish*, conversely, narrates an epic of war and struggle between the cosmic order and the forces of chaos, a struggle

23. Most of the following is taken from an excellent study, *Understanding Genesis: The Heritage of Biblical Israel*, by Nahum M. Sarna (New York: Schocken Books, 1972), pp. 11-23.

24. One is reminded of the first Greek philosopher, Thales of Miletus, who asserted that everything is water. From the Hindu scriptures, *Satapatha Brahmana*, the creation account reads, "Verily, in the beginning this universe was water, nothing but a sea of water. The waters desired, 'How can we be reproduced?' They toiled and performed fervid devotions." See *The Portable World Bible*, edited by Robert O. Ballou (New York, Penguin Books), p. 37. For other examples see the creation myths examined in *Mythologies of the Ancient World*, ed. S. N. Kramer (Garden City: Doubleday, 1961).

that was repeated annually in the life-cycle of nature in Mesopotamia. Finally, after a titanic struggle, Marduk establishes order in both nature and society.

4. In the Babylonian myth the deities fashion man as an afterthought, as a menial of the gods, a peon to provide them with nourishment and satisfy their physical needs. Genesis says God made man in His own image to control the creation and exploit the resources of nature (Gen. 1:26-29).

After careful comparison, therefore, you can clearly see that the Babylonian creation myth is closer to the theory of evolution than it is to the Biblical creation account! The gods of Babylon aren't really gods, since they arise later than nature and have no final control over natural forces. Ironic, isn't it, that one of the world's oldest creation stories is very similar to evolution? In both, nature is eternal, mechanistic, and dehumanizing.

Hence, if someone asks why we don't teach (say) the Buddhist theory of creation, I reply, "Because there is no Buddhist theory of creation! The Buddhists don't believe in creation; they teach that the universe is eternal!" It was no accident, therefore, that in the California textbook controversy in the early 1970's the Buddhists sided strongly with the evolutionists in keeping creation out of the books. They did so because their cosmology was already faithfully represented by the theory of evolution. Their worldview was already being taught in principle so why allow another worldview? It didn't seem to matter to them that both Buddhist cosmology and General Evolution were just as theological as creation.

It's a sad commentary on the intelligence of a nation when one religion gets its cosmology and theory of origins taught in school under the cover of being "scientific" while another religion has its view of ultimate origins prohibited. Perhaps in the near future an enlightened public will examine evolution as closely as it examined TM (Transcendental Meditation) and declare it to be religious and not truly scientific.

CREATION IS RELIGION, NOT SCIENCE

Our entire discussion had led to this point. We have alluded to this objection several times in the course of this book, and now we must take the bull by the horns. We devote the next chapter to this argument, which, in my judgment, is the most important of all.

5

WHEN DOES A THEORY BECOME RELIGIOUS?

When does a theory become religious? When does a hypothesis become theological? When does physics become metaphysics? When does history become metahistory? When does knowledge become faith? Once knowledge becomes faith is that faith still intellectually respectable?

These questions pinpoint one of the most persistent, nagging problems in the history of human thought: epistemology, the study of the sources, nature and tests of knowledge. For centuries thinkers have worried about the precise limits of human knowledge, about the precise boundary between the empirical and the super-empirical, between the natural and the supernatural. After a lengthy discussion, our current creation-evolution controversy ends with this ancient query.

A NEW LOOK AT AN OLD DISTINCTION

The champions of evolution insist that creation can't be taught in the public schools because it is religion, not science, and teaching it would therefore compromise the integrity of science. I maintain that scientists have already compromised the integrity of science by taking up the question of origins in the first place. They get into origins in the science classes and then find that they are unable to settle it decisively with the strict scientific method.

Then what do they do? Do they allow some other discipline to participate in the discussion of origins? No. Do they suspend judgment and admit that the problem is beyond science? No. They keep on teaching evolution, usually as fact, and vigorously beat down all attempts to investigate another solution. This is reprehensible and ought not to happen in a free society and in an academic institution.

All careful thinkers in this matter need to realize that no infallible person, no authoritative board, no Pope of Science, has ever defined precisely the boundary between physics and metaphysics. The boundary may turn out to be a foggy band rather than a precise line. Metaphysics (study of theories of reality) will never be as certain as physics (study of observable physical reality), but this doesn't mean that metaphysicians just take wild shots in the dark. We accept metaphysical systems because of their explanatory power, not because the systems themselves can be perfectly verified empirically. Worldviews recommend themselves by their clarity, consistency, coherence, and power to interpret.

The history of man illustrates that thinkers vary from epoch to epoch in their evaluation of the precise boundary between physics and metaphysics. Coates, White, and Schapiro observe that,

Modern historians and philosophers of science have shown that the actual course of scientific development does not depend alone upon the inner dialectic of the problems which scientists are studying at a particular time but depends also upon a dialectic between the community of scientists of a particular time and the cultural milieu within which they must operate. In many respects, the definition of what constitutes a specifically scientific as over against, say, a religious or aesthetic question, is prescientifically decided, that is to say, is decided by what scientists, influenced by the general cultural endowment of their society, agree to treat as susceptible to scientific scrutiny.[1]

For example, as recently as the last century, thinkers felt that human mental processes were not amenable to scientific investigation because scientists and nonscientists alike shared similar preconceptions about the special status of man in the animal kingdom. Today we seem to have no limits; we study almost everything with the scientific method. Or I should say, we *try* to study everything. Not everything lends itself to treatment by the strict scientific method, however, and origins appears to be a region where laboratory technique is severely limited.

A great deal of verbal legerdemain goes on when evolutionists argue that creation is not scientific. The discussion progresses until the evolutionist has defined the scientific method so narrowly that it is severely mechanistic and materialistic — matter is all we can allow to exist and it must operate automatically. This is all strict science will allow.

Now, if, after this narrow definition, you assert, "Creation is not a scientific theory," you are merely saying that creation is not mechanistic and materialistic. That's obvious. But

---

1. *The Emergence of Liberal Humanism,* Vol. I, *From the Renaissance to the French Revolution* (New York: McGraw-Hill, 1966), p. 145.

many laymen take the statement, "Creation is not a *scientific* theory," to mean, "Creation is not a *good* theory." Given the immense prestige of science in our culture, many unreflective people understand scientific to mean true, factual, or proved.

If evolutionists insist on keeping creation out of the discussion of origins because it is not science they must wake up to the fact that evolution is not really science either, at least by this narrow definition. As Ehrlich and Birch noted, it is "outside of empirical science." Karl Popper contends that the principle of natural selection is not a true scientific principle but is tautological and hence irrefutable. Philosophers like Antony Flew and Michael Scriven admit that evolution is more closely related to historical studies than to classic science. The prominent evolutionist, Ernst Mayr, concedes that classification of animal organisms is an "art," not a science. N. I. Platnick is very emphatic:

> Evolutionary biologists have a choice to make: either we agree with Mayr that narrative explanations are the name of the game, and continue drifting away from the rest of biology into an area ruled only by authority and consensus, or we insist that whenever possible our explanations be testable and potentially falsifiable and that evolutionary biology rejoin the scientific community at large.[2]

It should be noted, for comparison, that most creationists cheerfully admit creation is not strict science. Ariel Roth correctly observes that, "The concept of creation does not appear to meet the criterion of falsifiability any better than evolution. Science is not at its best when dealing with unique past events, whether these be considered as evolution or creation."[3]

---

2. For these and other revealing remarks from prominent evolutionists, see the excellent article by Ariel A. Roth, "Does Evolution Qualify as a Scientific Principle?" *Origins*, Vol. IV, No. 1, pp. 4-10.

3. *Ibid.*

It's not surprising that the same argument about falsification is used not only against creation but also against God. Antony Flew poses this challenge to believers in God: "What would have to have occurred to constitute for you a disproof of the love of, or the existence of God?"[4] Flew's point is that whatever is meaningful is also falsifiable. If the theist can't indicate how the universe would be different if there were no God at all, he can't use conditions in the universe as evidence that there is a God.

Flew's argument is flawed, however, because its demands are excessive. Not everything we assert must be empirically falsifiable — in fact, this very principle is itself incapable of empirical falsification. Our beliefs must be *testable* or *arguable*, for sure, but not empirically falsifiable. Human experience is such that this would be an excessive demand on the epistemology. If we should become omniscient . . . well, that would be a different ball game.

John Hick points out on Flew's argument that there is an asymmetrical relation between verifiability and falsifiability, that is, some assertions are falsified and verified in different ways. Take the question, "Am I immortal?" You could verify your own immortality if you consciously observed your own funeral. But you couldn't falsify your immortality because if you didn't survive death then you wouldn't be there to disprove your own survival. Furthermore, you couldn't empirically falsify another person's immortality because he might survive beyond your limited empirical knowledge.[5]

---

4. "Theology and Falsification," in *New Essays in Philosophical Thought,* edited by Antony Flew and Alasdair MacIntyre (London: SCM Press, 1955), p. 99.

5. See the careful discussion of this point in Norman Geisler, *Christian Apologetics* (Grand Rapids, Michigan: Baker Book House, 1976), p. 24.

THE REDUCTIVE FALLACY

In summary, I accuse the evolutionist of the Reductive Fallacy. You commit this fallacy when you "reduce" a complex thing or process to merely one of its parts or aspects, when you say that something complex is "merely" or "nothing but" this or that limited part of it. You are guilty of reductionism when you say things like, man is just an animal, the universe is nothing but matter, love is nothing but sex, music is merely sound waves.

More specifically, the evolutionist commits *methodological reductionism*. He defines the scientific method mechanistically and materialistically and then beats back all attempts to treat origins with any other approach.

Sir Arthur Eddington once used a priceless analogy that illustrates this fallacy. He says there once was a fisherman who concluded from his fishing experiments with a special net that, "No creation of the sea is less than two inches long." Now, this generalization disturbed some of his colleagues and they demurred, arguing that many sea creatures were certainly less than two inches and they just slipped through the holes in his special net. But the fisherman was unmoved. "What my net can't catch ain't fish," he pontificated and then scornfully accused his detractors of having pre-scientific, medieval, metaphysical prejudices.

Eddington's parable has a simple message: methodological reductionism can actually prevent an advance in knowledge. Two examples from the history of science will illustrate this.

1. Sigmund Freud was attracted to the study of the mind by the age-old malady of hysteria. For centuries doctors explained hysteria by merely dismissing it as unreal so that sufferers from hysterial symptoms were simply excluded from the arena of medical concern. In the Middle Ages this

alleged demon-mania caused people to charge hysterical people with witchcraft and have them tortured and burned.

Freud saw early on that hysteria was a "real sickness." Hysterical pain hurts just as much as real pain; hysterical blindness makes you just as unable to see as real blindness. Freud journeyed to Paris to continue his studies with the famous expert on hypnosis, Dr. Charcot, who at that time was proving that hypnosis could cause some of the same symptoms. Yet Dr. Charcot used a hypothesis that Freud found defective. He maintained that hysteria was simply a case of the physical nervous system degenerating.

To explain hysteria Freud broke with his colleagues and said it had a psychological, rather than a purely physiological, cause. Very early he suggested the hypothesis of Repression, the notion that something in the psychological mechanism of man is able to unconsciously forget many painful, unbearable, threatening, disturbing experiences. Freud pressed beyond reductive neurology in order to understand hysteria. His ideas enraged many of his colleagues. For example in Hamburg, 1910, at a meeting of neurologists, Professor Wilhelm Weygandt interrupted a discussion in which Freud's theory had been mentioned by banging his fist on the table and shouting, "This is not a topic for discussion at a scientific meeting; it is a matter for the police!"

At this fruitful juncture in the progress of human knowledge a methodological reductionist would have exclaimed: "Sigmund stop! Sigmund, you can't possibly explain hysteria that way! You must explain it by some neurological process. If you get beyond the physical nervous system you get into metaphysics and the supernatural where you can't check anything." Freud probably would have replied: "I must explain hysteria by what makes sense and what works.

I can't understand it without going beyond the nervous system."[6]

2. Wilder Penfield of McGill University studied the human brain for many decades. He carried out numerous experiments on the exposed brains of conscious, consenting patients who were undergoing operations. Penfield applied low-voltage currents to selected points on the surface of the cerebral cortex. The patient was unaware of the current but he saw the movement it caused him to execute. Often when Penfield would cause a hand to move and ask the patient why he moved his hand, the patient would reply, "I didn't do it. You made me do it!" The patient obviously thought of himself as having somehow an existence separate from his own body. Penfield wrote:

> Once when I warned such a patient of my intention to stimulate the motor areas of the cortex, and challenged him to keep his hand from moving when the electrode was applied, he seized it with the other hand and struggled to hold it still. Thus, one hand, under the control of the right hemisphere driven by an electrode, and the other hand, which he controlled through the left hemisphere, were caused to struggle against each other. Behind the "brain action" of one hemisphere was the patient's mind. Behind the action of the other hemisphere was the electrode.[7]

Toward the end of his life Penfield summarized the philosophical implications of his research in a book, *The Mystery*

---

6. See David Stafford-Clark, *What Freud Really Said* (New York: Schocken Books, 1966), pp. 17-30. Lastrucci alludes to Freud's theory of "unconscious motivation" as an example of theories "so abstract as to defy deduction of fruitful (i.e. empirically testable) hypotheses" (*The Scientific Approach,* p. 115).

7. See Penfield's paper delivered at the "Control of the Mind" Symposium held at the University of California Medical Center in San Francisco, 1961, quoted in Arthur Koestler, *The Ghost in the Machine* (New York: Macmillan, 1967), p. 203. See also Penfield's article, "Memory Mechanism," *A.M.A. Archives of Neurology and Psychiatry,* 67 (1952), pp. 178-198.

of the Mind. Here he noted that his research forced him to give up his physical monism and adopt a psycho-physical dualism to understand how people behaved when he probed their brains. "After a professional lifetime spent in trying to discover how the brain accounts for the mind," he says, "it comes as a surprise now to discover, during this final examination of the evidence, that the dualist hypothesis seems the more reasonable of the two possible explanations." He then writes in a personal vein:

> Since every man must adopt for himself, without the help of science, his way of life and his personal religion, I have long had my own private beliefs. What a thrill it is, then, to discover that the scientist, too, can legitimately believe in the existence of the spirit![8]

A methodological reductionist would dispute this conclusion. He would say that Penfield should have kept on looking (forever, I suppose) until he had found the explanation of human behavior in the physical brain. The quotation above indicates that Penfield believed his personal religion was "beyond science," but notice also that he felt such belief was "legitimate."

Were Freud and Penfield compromising the integrity of science? Were they justified in pressing beyond monistic materialism and venturing into the trans-empirical? I think so. To stick with mere neurology when the facts cry out for something beyond seems intellectually perverse, like Eddington's fisherman who said, "What my net can't catch ain't fish."

CONCLUSION

We find, therefore, that when the evolutionist opposes creation because it is religion and not science, he is exploiting

---

8. *The Mystery of the Mind,* (Princeton University Press), 1975, p. 85.

two things: (1) the ambiguity of terms like religion and science, and (2) the faulty public understanding of a crucial epistemological issue. If empirical verification and/or falsification be required for scientific theories then evolution must be excluded from science classes along with creation.

If one wishes to define science in a narrow, mechanistic, materialistic way that's fine, I suppose, but don't teach evolution after you define it because evolution isn't science by that narrow definition. It is, rather, *evolutionism*! It belongs in a different kind of class, the same class where creation is discussed.

6

CONCLUSION

I hope that this short essay has stimulated the reader to some constructive thought on the current creation-evolution controversy. We can rectify the present injustice in the teaching of origins by simply implementing a policy where both models are taught in a context of mutual respect for each other and for the limitations of the strict, empirical scientific method.

In the 1970's there has been an explosion of private schools in America. The reasons for public disenchantment with public education are many — crime, violence, sex, drugs, poor academic standards — but one of the reasons often given for this disenchantment is the unfair way that origins is taught.

I suggest (one last time!) that both creation and evolution be investigated in classes like "Theories of Origins," just as we have classes called, "Theories of Personality," and "Theories of History." If science instructors keep teaching evolution in science classes as established fact that will be intellectually dishonest, academically lamentable, and politically indefensible.

We close by repeating the words of Clarence Darrow: "It is bigotry for public schools to teach only one theory of origins."

SUGGESTIONS FOR FURTHER READING

(1) Books by creationist scientists emphasizing the scientific aspects of creationism.

Bales, James and R. T. Clark. *Why Scientists Accept Evolution.* Nutley, N.J.: Presbyterian and Reformed, 1966.

Coder, S. Maxwell and George F. Howe. *The Bible, Science and Creation.* Chicago: Moody Press, 1965.

Coppedge, James. *Evolution: Possible or Impossible?* Grand Rapids: Zondervan, 1973.

Gish, Duane T. *Speculations and Experiments on the Origin of Life.* San Diego: Institute for Creation Research, 1972.

_____. *Evolution? The Fossils Say No!*, 3rd ed. San Diego: Creation-Life Books, 1979.

Klotz, John W. *Genes, Genesis, and Evolution,* rev. ed. St. Louis: Concordia, 1970.

Lammerts, W. E. ed. *Why Not Creation?* Philadelphia: Presbyterian and Reformed, 1970.

_____. *Scientific Studies in Special Creation.* Philadelphia: Presbyterian and Reformed, 1971.

Moore, John N. *Questions and Answers on Creation and Evolution.* Grand Rapids: Baker Book House, 1976.

Moore, John N. and Harold S. Slusher, eds. *Biology: A Search for Order in Complexity,* 2nd ed. Grand Rapids: Zondervan, 1974.

Morris, Henry M. and John C. Whitcomb. *The Genesis Flood.* Philadelphia: Presbyterian and Reformed, 1961.

Shute, Evan. *Flaws in the Theory of Evolution.* Philadelphia: Presbyterian and Reformed, 1966.

Smith, A. E. Wilder. *The Creation of Life.* Wheaton, Illinois: Harold Shaw Publishers, 1970.

_____. *Man's Origin, Man's Destiny.* Wheaton, Illinois: Harold Shaw Publishers, 1968.

(2) Books by evolutionists containing valuable critiques of aspects of evolutionary theory or practice.

Barzun, Jacques. *Darwin, Marx, Wagner: Critique of a Heritage.* New York: Doubleday, 1958.

Himmelfarb, Gertrude. *Darwin and the Darwinian Revolution.* London: Chatto and Windus, 1959.

Kerkut, G. A. *Implications of Evolution.* London: Pergamon Press, 1960.

MacBeth, Norman. *Darwin Retried.* Boston: Gambit, 1971.

Moorhead, P. S. and M. M. Kaplan, eds. *Mathematical Challenges to the Neo-Darwinian Interpretation of Evolution.* Philadelphia: Wistar Institute Press, 1967.

(3) Books by evolutionists presenting evolution as a fact or as the only possible theory of origins.

Ames, Robert and Philip Siegelman. *The Idea of Evolution.* Minneapolis: Meyers, 1957.

Beck, William S. and George G. Simpson. *Life: An Introduction to Biology.* New York: Harcourt, Brace, and World, 1965.

Dobzhansky, Theodosius. *Evolution, Genetics and Man.* New York: John Wiley and Sons, 1955.

Goldschmidt, Richard. *The Material Basis for Evolution.* New Haven: Yale University Press, 1940.

Huxley, Julian. *Evolution in Action.* New York: Harper and Brothers, 1953.

Moody, Paul A. *Introduction to Evolution,* 2nd ed. New York: Harper and Row, 1962.

Simpson, George G. *Tempo and Mode in Evolution.* New York: Columbia University Press, 1944.

_____. *The Major Features of Evolution.* New York: Simon and Schuster, 1953.

_____. *The Meaning of Evolution.* New Haven: Yale University Press, 1949.